Church and Climate Justice

Reimagining Church as Event: Perspectives from the Margins
Series Editors: George Zachariah and Sudipta Singh

In these eleven volumes, a collective of Indian theologians envisions Church as an Event that happens in particular contexts in the life of the communities at the margins. They argue that in the life of the communities who experience on their bodies the violence and hegemony of dominant power relations, morality, and religious dogmas and practices, the church happens as countercultural experiences that disrupt the logic of the prevailing order. These experiences enable and empower them to affirm and celebrate their differences, knowledges and beauty even as they weave their liberation. Church as event is a call to rising to life, creating life-flourishing communities that live out the foretaste of the reign of God.

Titles in this Series

Church and Religious Diversity Joshua Samuel and Samuel Mall
Church and Gender Justice Aruna Gnanadason
Faith in the Age of Empire Y.T. Vinayaraj
Dalitekklesia: A Church from Below Raj Bharat Patta
Church and Climate Justice Vinod Wesley
Church and Disability Samuel George
Church and Diakonia in the Age of COVID-19 Mothy Varkey
Decolonising Oikoumene Gladson Jathanna
Church and Human Sexuality Arvind Theodore
With Many Voices: Liturgies in Context Viji Varghese Eapen (Ed.)
The Word becoming Flesh George Zachariah

Church and Climate Justice

Vinod Wesley

2020

Church and Climate Justice- jointly published by the Indian Society for Promoting Christian Knowledge (ISPCK), Post Box 1585, Kashmere Gate, Delhi-110006 and Council for World Mission, Singapore-338729.

Online order: http://ispck.org.in/book.php

Also available on amazon.in

ISBN: 978-93-88945-86-8

Kindle Edition: 978-93-88945-98-1

Cover Illustration Credit : Immanuel Paul Vivekanandh K

Laser typeset by

ISPCK, Post Box 1585, 1654, Madarsa Road, Kashmere Gate, Delhi-110006 • *Tel:* 23866323

e-mail: ashish@ispck.org.in • ella@ispck.org.in
website: www.ispck.org.in

Dedicated to
My Parents
Rev. John Wesley and Rev. Vimala Wesley

Contents

Foreword

DISCERNMENT AND RADICAL ENGAGEMENT (DARE) is an initiative of the Council for World Mission (CWM) to enable faith communities to *clarify what it means to engage in* public witness to God's justice and peace in a corrupt and conflicted world.

> The mission of DARE is conceived as the coming together of (a) the *radical soul* of discernment and sense-making in theology and biblical criticism; (b) the yearnings for *signifying engagement* that rise out of the slums of modernism and the valleys of despair; and (c) the commitment to redemption songs that *inspire disturbance* at the hubs of power.

As part of the DARE initiative, each region of CWM is invited to prepare and share biblical and theological resources on current themes and issues being considered by CWM, drawing upon the experiences and resources from the region.

Interfaith Engagement, Ecumenism and Inclusive communities against dehumanising social categorisations are the themes for the book series undertaken by the South Asia region of CWM. The thrust is centred on **Reimagining Church as Event: Perspectives from the Margins**. It calls to the fore persons living in the margins and highlights their voice, their narratives and their passion for a rearrangement of life in communities, as we know it, and a commitment to rise to life and to break out from Babylon. These books are intended for the use of lay people, pastors and evangelists as well as for theological students and seminaries. The series offer stories and narratives, analyses, liturgical resources, biblical, theological and ethical reflections, and missional/praxis proposals.

Church is an event that happens at the margins of contemporary life. Church happens as an epiphanic event where the divine presence is manifested and experienced in the pathos, struggles, contestations and harmonies of everyday existence. Church happens in those spaces where we celebrate the presence of Jesus, the Christ, in the flourishing of life. Church happens when we are transformed by one another, and inspired and enabled to engage in the transformative politics of the reign of God. Church happens whenever and wherever spirit-filled communities reclaim their subversive moral agency and contest the logic and practices of domination and exclusion. Church happens when the community experiences the healing power of the wounded healer and join Jesus in this risk-taking mission, despite the wounds we bear. To reimagine Church requires courage and commitment to engage in the mission of nurturing and organising communities of resistance and healing. This book series is a humble attempt at exposing and encouraging this radical expression of Church.

I appreciate and thank all those who are associated with this series, the authors, the contributors, the publishers and the editors. I commend this book series in the hope and prayers that they will help the faith communities in South Asia, and beyond, to *discern God's presence in community and dare to engage* in ways that re-present the God of life in communities and in the public square, *Rising to Life: Living out the New Heaven and New Earth.*

Colin Cowan
General Secretary
Council for World Mission

Introduction

*Geevarghese Coorilos Nalunnakkal**

Let me quote a few lines from a poem by Kathy Jentil-Kijiner, poet and climate activist from Marshall Islands, which she has dedicated to her little daughter Matafele Peinam:

> *And now there are thousands out*
> *on the street marching with signs*
> *hand in hand*
> *chanting for change NOW*

Indeed, it is "Now or Never." The future of our planet and life thereof will depend on how human race is going to respond to the challenge of climate change. It has been predicted that global warming is all set to increase up to 1.5 degree Celsius between 2030 and 2050 and that this will result in extreme weather patterns and related disasters of extraordinary magnitude such as floods, droughts, cyclones, wildfires, hurricanes, earthquakes and even pandemics of new versions and proportions. When this book, *Church and Climate Change,* was completed, the COVID-19 epidemic had not made its entry. The deadly connection between pandemics such as COVID-19 and environmental factors is nothing new, but in the context of worsening climate change,

COVID-19 could well be nature's latest (in all probability not the last) and perhaps the strongest alarm bell against climate change. Climate change, amongst other things, has the potential to cascade disasters with immense socio-economic and other ramifications such as food shortage, poverty, migration, conflicts over resources, and refugee crisis. All this is already evident in many parts of the world, particularly in the Global South. Even more serious is the concern that climate change has the potential to make these problems permanent. This makes climate change above all a justice concern as the immediate victims of climate change are the poorest of the poor. Worse still is the fact that those who are forced to bear the real brunt of it all have practically no role in causing climate change. It is from this vantage point, through the lens of justice, the perspective of victims, that Vinod Wesley approaches climate change in his book, *Church and Climate Change*.

When I started my doctoral research on the integral connection between socio-economic-gender justice and environmental justice (eco-justice) and its theological and ethical implications for the church and wider society and eventually published my findings in a book form in the 1990s (*Green Liberation: Towards an Integral Ecotheology*), I had to face criticism even from my progressive colleagues that it was a luxury for the Global South to address environmental issues as it was deemed an elitist concern by progressive theologians in the 1980s and 1990s. Today, though, liberation theologies have travelled a long way in recognising the vital link between environmental exploitation and poverty; between alienation of nature and marginalisation of the poor, particularly of indigenous peoples and their womenfolk. The ground-breaking critique of Lynn White Jr. (1967) that the Christian theological anthropocentrism, implicit in its creation narratives that seem to accord humanity a certain 'dominion' over the rest of creation and similar warnings from other quarters, also meant that theology really mattered. These have also challenged progressive theologies like liberation theology to move beyond the world of human history and take ecological concerns much more seriously. There have been several attempts in liberation theology to articulate theology and ethics from this integral perspective of eco-justice ever since. Said this, it must be added that the specific issue of climate change has not been given sufficient attention by churches and theologians. *Church and Climate Change* will surely go a long way in bridging this glaring gap.

There have been different theological approaches to climate change. Forrest Clingerman and Kevin J. O'Brien introduce two contrasting approaches. The school that looks at climate change as *sui generis*, as a brand new problem that requires novel thinking and response, appears to embrace the inevitability of apocalyptic change, increasing instability, and an Anthropocene age that calls for a new kind of religion and spirituality. On the other hand, those who see climate change as prefigured by the biggest events in human history such as the moral crime of slavery tend to highlight a renewed relevance of religious traditions, especially their commitment to social justice and their opposition to unjust and destructive structures of political and economic order.

Vinod Wesley here talks about three dominant strands: those of denial, fatalism, and justice. The first approach simply dismisses the claim that climate change exists. The second strand tends to consider issues such as climate change as inevitable signs of the *eschaton*. However, the author here, already indicated, follows the justice paradigm that makes appeals to the liberative strands within the Christian theological tradition. Issues of climate change, therefore, become climate justice concerns in the theological discourse that is offered in the book. From this liberation perspective, the author brings in the Bible, theology, ethics and mission of the church in dialogue. The author has made a commendable effort in bringing on board the contemporary literature and resources on the issue, drawing on scholarship from both Global South and North and also from various ecclesial traditions.

The highlight of the book, to me, is the prophetic tone and content of the book. "Prophetic imagination," to use an expression that Walter Brueggemann has popularised, runs through the book. As *Song of the Prophets: A Global Theology of Climate Change*, a Christian Aid publication puts it, prophets are those who offer the most scathing critique of unjust systems that exploit people and their environment. They also hold signs of hope that is rooted in the promise of God. Wesley, standing in the true prophetic tradition, offers both a critique of the unjust systems in our church and society, and genuine signs of hope in the form of alternative visions of church and social movements that stand and fight for justice, peace and integrity of creation. Prophetic voices are revolutionary songs and slogans. *Church and Climate Change* by Wesley is certainly one such prophetic voice that we must lend our ears to.

May I also take this opportunity to congratulate Vinod Wesley, the author of the book, on such a relevant publication on one of the most pertinent and pressing issues of our times. I also wish him all God's blessings in his future ministry and academic career. I should also like to offer my sincere gratitude to my ecumenical colleague and friend Mr. Sudipta Singh and the Council for World Mission (CWM) for offering me the honour and privilege to write these introductory remarks. My hope is that this book and others in the series will enjoy wide readership.

*Geevarghese Coorilos Nalunnakkal is the Metropolitan of the Malankara Jacobite Syrian Orthodox Church. He also serves as the Moderator of the Commission on World Mission and Evangelism of the World Council of Churches.

Acknowledgements

This book is a dream come true in my theological journey. I have been thinking for a long time to write a book on climate change for churches. I thank the DARE initiative of the Council for World Mission for making this possible. My special thanks to Dr. Sudipta Singh. I thank my friend and mentor Dr. George Zachariah for his inputs and valuable comments at various stages of writing this book.

I want to extend my gratitude to the Gurukul Lutheran Theological College, Chennai, the Union Theological Seminary, New York, and the Lutheran School of Theology at Chicago. These institutions enriched and groomed me theologically. I thank all my professors who have imparted significant knowledge on climate change from theological and ethical perspectives.

I am very grateful to the churches that shaped my faith and continue to encourage me to bear witness in the public sphere on justice issues. I extend my deep gratitude to the Church of South India, the Trinity Episcopal Church at Wall Street, New York, and the Chicago Tamil Church (UCC) for constantly reminding me to live out the gospel values in the context of climate injustice.

I am indebted to several grassroots movements, activists and theologians who have been a great inspiration and source for this book.

I am indebted to my parents, Rev. John Wesley and Rev. Vimala Wesley, who groomed me in the Christian faith and for encouraging me to work on this project.

This book would have not been possible without the wonderful support, love and encouragement from my wife Kiruba Immanuel. I also thank my daughter Tanya Adelyn for her smiles and hugs which gave me a lot of energy in writing this book.

Chapter 1

Climate Change: An Introduction

Changes in weather patterns and ecological disasters have been part of human life for centuries. The twenty-first century is marked by many occurrences of ecological disasters that have proven to be caused by human action altering the earth's climate. South Asian countries have a large number of people who are victims to climate change today. A World Bank report titled "South Asia's Hotspots" points out that around 800 million people (half of South Asia's population) live in areas that are severely affected due to climate change. Extreme events of drought, floods, heat waves, storms and sea-level rise have greatly impacted the South Asian community. Changing climate has also altered the living conditions in India, Pakistan, Bangladesh, Sri Lanka, Afghanistan, Nepal and the Maldives. There is an urgent need to intensify the efforts to address climate change and to support the work of mitigating and adapting to climate change. At this juncture, the church has to deeply recognise its call to dedicate and involve itself in the mission to protect the created world of God and the vulnerable communities and challenge the economic and political forces that cause this climate change.

This book is an attempt to help churches to have a better understanding of climate change and to provide a biblical, theological, ethical and ecclesiological approach to committing itself to address the issue of climate change. This book has six chapters. This chapter defines climate change, examines its consequence on lives and livelihoods, and emphasises the need for a Christian response to the challenge posed by it. The second chapter focuses on how the Bible is an important resource to address climate change. The third chapter is about climate change and Christian theology/doctrines. Many theologians have addressed the issue of climate change which helps the church to redefine its faith in the context of climate crisis. The fourth chapter focuses on women, who are the worst victims of climate change but at the same time are active agents of change. The fifth chapter is on Christian ethical reflections on climate change. Here, the concepts of eco-justice and climate justice are discussed from a Third World perspective. The last chapter maps out the responsibilities of the church in its praxis towards climate concerns today. This book also has a Bible study from the Book of Revelation and a liturgy for worship to celebrate God's creation and to recommit ourselves to renew the world in the context of the present climate crisis.

What is Climate Change?

Climate change is defined, in a NASA document on global climate change, as a long-term change in the average weather patterns that have come to define the earth's local, regional and global climates. The term 'weather' refers to atmospheric conditions that occur locally over short periods from a few minutes to hours or days, like rain, snow, clouds, winds, floods or thunderstorms. The term, climate, on the other hand, refers to the long-term regional or global temperature, humidity and rainfall patterns over seasons, years or decades.[1]

The changes in climate since the early twentieth century have been attributed primarily to fossil fuel burning. Fossil fuel burning increases the greenhouse gas levels in the atmosphere, raising the earth's average surface temperature. These temperature variations are referred to as global warming.

Since the pre-industrial time, human activities are estimated to have increased the earth's global average temperature by about 1 degree Celsius (1.8 ^{0}Fahrenheit). The temperature has increased by 0.2 ^{0}C (0.36 ^{0}F) every decade. Experts say that since the 1950s the extent of warming because of human activity has accelerated.[2]

Natural processes also contribute to climate change (e.g., ocean patterns like El Niño, La Niña, and the Pacific decadal oscillation, volcanic activity, changes in the sun's energy output, and so on). But there is a clear distinction between climate change attributable to human activities and to natural causes.

The Intergovernmental Panel for Climate Change (IPCC) is the United Nations body for assessing the science related to climate change. It defines climate and climate change as follows:[3]

Climate

The climate in a narrow sense is usually defined as the average weather, or more rigorously, as the statistical description in terms of the mean and variability of relevant quantities over a period ranging from months to thousands or millions of years. The classical period for averaging these variables is 30 years, as defined by the World Meteorological Organization. The relevant quantities are most often surface variables such as temperature, precipitation and wind. Climate in a wider sense is the state, including a statistical description, of the climate system.

Climate Change

Climate change refers to a change in the state of the climate that can be identified (e.g., by using statistical tests) by changes in the mean and/or the variability of its properties and that persists for an extended period, typically decades or longer. Climate change may be due to natural internal processes or external forcings such as modulations of the solar cycles, volcanic eruptions and persistent anthropogenic changes in the composition of the atmosphere or land use. ...The Framework Convention on Climate Change (UNFCCC), in its Article 1, defines climate change as: 'a change of climate which is attributed directly or indirectly to human activity that alters the composition of the global atmosphere and which is in addition to natural climate variability observed over comparable time periods.' The UNFCCC thus makes a distinction between climate change attributable to human activities altering the atmospheric composition and climate variability attributable to natural causes.

Greenhouse gases caused by human activities, largely for its economic development, form the main reason for climate change. The gases that contribute to the enhanced greenhouse effect are carbon dioxide (CO_2), chlorofluorocarbons (CFCs), methane (CH_4) and nitrous oxide (N_2O) emitted from the combustion of fossil fuels, deforestation and agriculture, and sulphur hexafluoride (SF_6) and perfluorocarbons arising from industrial processes. As a percentage of the greenhouse gases, CO_2 is the highest, followed by CH_4, CFCs, N_2O and others (like halons, tropospheric ozone, sulphur hexafluoride, among others). Some other gases, including carbon monoxide, nitrogen oxides and volatile organic compounds, contribute indirectly to global warming through chemical reactions in the atmosphere. Other emissions, such as sulfate aerosols, have a cooling or dimming effect on the climate as they reflect some of the short-wave radiation before it reaches the earth's surface.

The Impact of Climate Change

The IPCC's *Special Report on Global Warming of 1.5 °C* is considered one of the authentic scientific reports on climate change. Prepared by 91 authors from 40 countries, it includes over 6,000 scientific references, and was published on 8 October 2018. The report was delivered at the United Nations' 48th session of the IPCC to deliver the authoritative, scientific guide for governments to deal with climate change. The report gives us the compelling realities of climate change and urges nations to take necessary action. According to it, human activities have caused 1.0 °C of global warming above pre-industrial levels and it will increase to 1.5 °C between 2030 and 2052. This will cause extreme weather conditions, heavy precipitation and severe droughts. There will be a mega sea-level rise by 2100. It will increase ocean acidity and decrease ocean oxygen levels. It will have climate-related risks to health, livelihood and food security.[4]

Milburn Thompson, the author of *Justice and Peace: A Christian Primer,* gives several evidences of the effects of climate change on the natural world and human lives. In August 2000, in a phenomenon that has not occurred for fifty million years and never witnessed by humans before, the North Pole melted. The ten hottest years—the hottest year records began in 1880—have all been since 2003 with the exception of 1998. The hottest year since then was 2016. In 2016, the amount of CO_2 in the atmosphere climbed to its highest level in 800,000 years. The sea-ice extent in the Antarctic was at a record low in 2016.[5]

The impacts of climate change are different in different places. But significantly, it is the poor countries that bear the brunt of climate change since they do not have the economic resources to prevent or to recover from ecological disasters. Countries like Bangladesh, many island communities and sub-Saharan Africa are affected more than others because of climate change. Thompson points out that in the two decades between 1995 and 2015, weather-related disasters killed 606,000 people; left 4.1 billion people injured, homeless, or in need of emergency treatment; and cost more than $1.9 trillion. There was an average of 335 weather-related disasters every year over these two decades, twice the rate in the previous ten years. Weather-related disasters affected developed and developing countries too, with the United States and China reporting the most number of events, but in these countries too it is the poor that were the most harmed by the disasters.[6]

According to Thompson, Bangladesh, which produces only 0.3 per cent of the emissions in the world, is a striking example of the plight of developing countries and the poorest people facing the impact of climate change caused by others. A densely populated area of about 160 million, it is one of the worst-affected communities of climate change, especially due to the rising level of seawater. The saltwater of the rising seas intrudes into rivers, making the water brackish and poisoning the fields. Because of the rise in sea levels the cities are also sinking. Several storms and cyclones have washed away the houses of the poor. It is projected that by 2050, rising sea levels will inundate 17 per cent of the land and create fifty million Bangladeshi environmental refugees.[7]

Droughts, hurricanes, cyclones and typhoons have increased a lot and have affected people all over the globe. Hurricane

Katrina devastated New Orleans in 2005, Superstorm Sandy wreaked havoc from Cuba to Maine in 2012, Typhoon Haiyan killed more than 6,300 people and left around 11 million people homeless in the Philippines in 2013.[8]

These disasters caused by climate change also lead to a lot of deforestation. For instance, Hurricane Katrina destroyed or damaged an estimated 320 million trees across the Gulf coast, containing about 100 millions of carbon. Hurricane Maria, which struck Puerto Rico in September 2017, devastated some 30 million trees.[9]

Human Role in Climate Change

In its periodic assessments, the IPCC has been affirming that human activity is the principal cause for global warming and climate change. In 1990, the IPCC said that emissions from human activities were "substantially increasing" greenhouse gas concentrations in the atmosphere, which would lead to global warming. By 2013, the panel had concluded that, "It is extremely likely that human influence has been the dominant cause of the observed warming since the mid-20th century."[10]

The Centre for Climate and Energy Solutions, a non-profit organisation in Arlington, Virginia, US, working to forge practical solutions to climate change, has systematically summarised the affirmation in various IPCC reports of the human role in climate change. The following statements in the assessment reports are an indictment of the impact of human activities causing climate change: "…Emissions resulting from human activities are substantially increasing atmospheric concentrations of greenhouse gases" (1990, First Assessment report); "There is new and stronger evidence that most of the warming observed over the last 50 years is attributable to human activities" (2001,

Third Assessment); "Most of the observed increase in global average temperatures since the mid-20th century is very likely due to the observed increase in anthropogenic greenhouse gas concentrations" (2007, Fourth Assessment); and, "It is extremely likely that human influence has been the dominant cause of the observed warming since the mid-20th century."[11]

South Asia as a Vulnerable Region

South Asia is highly vulnerable to climate change because of its varied geographical location and diverse climatic conditions. The "South Asia's Hotspots" report points out how the changes in seasonal rainfall have already affected the agricultural system across South Asia. Due to the increase in cyclones in the Indian Ocean, Bangladesh and the Maldives are increasingly vulnerable to flooding.[12] This report goes on to mention that urban places like Dhaka, Karachi, Kolkata and Mumbai which together account for a population of more than 50 million face a high risk of flood-related damage. There has also been significant increase in temperature by 1 °C to 3 °C (1.8 °F to 5.4 °F) in Western Afghanistan and southwestern Pakistan from 1950 to 2010. During the same period, there has been an increase of 1 °C to 1.5 °C (1.8 °F to 2.7 °F) in southeastern India, western Sri Lanka, northern Pakistan and eastern Nepal.[13]

According to the IPCC's Fifth Assessment Report, diseases have been increasing in South Asian countries because of the rise in temperature. High temperature and heavy rainfall cause pathogens and parasites to multiply faster, which has led to diarrhoea and cholera outbreaks in many places in South Asia. Studies have associated cholera epidemics in Bangladesh to climate change.[14] For instance, experts say, climate-induced warming of the earth makes possible the growth of various algae and bacteria, leading to more cholera cases in the country.

It is also highly predicted that a rise of 2-4 ^{0}C will have drastic effects on agriculture, leading to food insecurity, especially in rural areas.[15] Nearly 70 per cent of the 1.8 billion population in South Asia depends on agriculture. Failure in agriculture and food production will cause huge migration and food crisis.

Climate change-induced human migration is also a common reality in South Asian countries. It is believed that in Bangladesh alone 15 million people will be displaced due to climate-related disasters in their coastal areas.[16] Large migrations happen between Bangladesh and India, Afghanistan and Pakistan, and Nepal and India. Climate-induced migrants are mostly from poor backgrounds. Moreover, when the host country is itself under severe crisis due to climate change, the presence of migrants creates a lot of tension with the local community. This has led to several violent conflicts in many areas. The migrants who are forced to leave their country because of the loss of their livelihood thus end up in a more dangerous situation in the place to which they have migrated.

According to the Global Climate Risk Index by Germanwatch, a development and environmental organisation which lobbies for sustainable global development, Pakistan is the seventh most vulnerable country to climate change. Pakistan saw severe drought in the southern regions in Sindh province in 1998-2002 and 2014-17.[17] As a result of climate change, Pakistan has been witnessing a number of floods and long spells of drought which is creating a major water scarcity for its people.

Pakistan's high mountains have some of the world's most important glaciers—almost 5,000 glaciers. Warming climate causes difficult and dangerous living conditions for the people living in the valley. The valley of Bagrote in Gilgit-Baltistan, for instance, is home to half a dozen glaciers which are on the verge of melting. Such melting of glaciers have led to glacial floods in the mountainous regions of Khyber Pakhtunkhwa and Gilgit-Baltistan. Of 3,044 glacial lakes, it is estimated that 33 are likely to result in glacial lake outburst floods. Such flooding will result in releasing millions of cubic metres of water and debris that will affect the lives of more than seven million people living in northern Pakistan.[18]

The Maldives is considered a paradise in south Asia. It is a picturesque chain of more than 1,100 islands and atolls in the Indian Ocean. But increasing sea level could soon submerge the country. Since the highest parts of the Maldives rise to more than eight feet, this would leave nearly 400,000 residents at risk of storm surges and rising seas. The December 2004 Indian Ocean tsunami led to considerable damage here, disrupting freshwater supplies and damaging homes in many parts of the islands. Moreover, extreme mining of the protective sand and coral around the islands has made them more vulnerable to rising waters. Scientists predict that the beautiful coral atolls of the Maldives may by 2050 submerge into the sea and disappear.[19]

Bhutan, a part of the Eastern Himalayas, has pride of place in South Asia as a carbon-neutral region. It is a small country with glaciers, snow-capped mountains, a large forest cover and rich biodiversity. But Bhutan is not immune from the effect of global warming trends. There is the threat of outburst floods in Bhutan and the Eastern Himalayas from at least 22 potentially dangerous glacial lakes.[20] This poses a serious threat to areas lying downstream. Though Bhutan follows environmentally sustainable economy and conservative approaches to living, it is still a victim of climate change. A highly a water-dependent economy, Bhutan thrives on hydropower, agriculture and tourism. The greatest challenge in the future from climate change will be to its water security.

Sri Lanka has a land area of 65,610 square kilometres and a coastline of 1,340 km. Nearly half of the inhabitants of the 22 million population live in the west, south-west, and southern coasts of the island. More than 21 per cent of the population is still engaged in agriculture and over 145,000 thousand people depend on fisheries. Extreme dry season, heavy rains and floods periodically disrupt life in the coastal regions and of those involved in agriculture.

Warming of the oceans will cause migration of fishes which will affect a large number of people involved in the fishing industry. In 2017, Sri Lanka was ranked the second most impacted territory of events such as storms, floods and heat waves, entailing extreme loss of human lives and property.[21] Sri Lanka's close proximity to the ocean makes it more vulnerable to extreme tropical storms and sea-level rise. Studies have suggested that almost 19 million people in Sri Lanka live in hotspots of climate change. If the carbon emission continues at the same pace, 90 per cent of the population is likely to be in that scenario by 2050.[22] Apart from this, extreme climatic conditions increase vector and waterborne diseases such as malaria, dengue, diarrhoea, and leptospirosis. What ensues from poverty, loss of property and human lives are psychological problems in the community.

India is one of the most climate vulnerable countries around the globe and in South Asia. The highly diverse climate, ranging from the subfreezing Himalayan winters to the tropical climate of the south, makes the climate change impact more complex. In the past 30 years, economic losses from weather-related events have doubled. Ten of the 14 extreme weather-related disasters between 1998 and 2017 have cost approximately $45 billion. Over 27,000 people have died and 370 million people have been affected.[23] In 2018, the prolonged southwest monsoon over the state of Kerala resulted in one of the worst floods India has ever experienced in 100 years. Apart from unimaginable loss (estimated at $4.25 billion), more than 800,000 people were displaced and 400 people lost their lives.[24]

India has a large number of people who are displaced due to climate disaster. As many as 2.7 million of the 3.3 million people displaced in South Asia due to storms and floods in 2018 were in India.[25] According to the State of India's Environment 2020 report, published on 9 February 2020, India recorded just nine out of 93 disasters in Asia in 2019 but accounted for nearly 48 per cent of the deaths. According to the National Disaster Management Authority in the country, 27 of the 37 states and Union Territories in India are disaster-prone.[26]

Climate Change and Christian Response

There have been different responses from the Christian community to climate change. There are climate-deniers who say climate change is not real. Some of them believe that the destruction of the world is preordained according to the Bible and that climate change only proves that the end of the world is near (eschatology). On the other hand, there are a large number of people who challenge human greed that exploits the created order and the neoliberal capitalist economic structures that propel industrialisation, which ultimately alter the climate patterns.

This particular book is an attempt towards such a justice-oriented response from a South Asian perspective. Environmental issues and climate change are not merely economic issues but also religio-political and ethical issues. Many of us are part of causing climate change and several of us are victims of climate change. Today environmental issues are theological, philosophical and ethical as much as they are scientific, technological, economic and political. This is an important moment for the South Asian church to engage prophetically in challenging the socio-economic and political forces that lead to the exploitation of nature and the theology and faith that support them.

Endnotes

[1] https://climate.nasa.gov/resources/global-warming-vs-climate-change/, accessed on 3 Jan 2020.

[2] https://climate.nasa.gov/resources/global-warming-verse-climate-change/, accessed on 3 Jan 2020.

[3] The definitions of Climate and Climate change are taken from the glossary section of the IPCC which has several scientifically based definitions on climate concerns. https://www.ipcc.ch/sr15/chapter/glossary/ accessed on 3 Jan 2020.

[4] https://www.ipcc.ch/site/assets/uploads/sites/2/2019/06/SR15_Headline-statements.pdf, accessed on 20 Jan 2020.

[5] Milburn Thomson takes these facts from resources like The American Association for the Advancement of Science (AAAS) and the National Oceanic and Atmospheric Administration (NOAA). J. Milburn Thompson, *Justice and Peace A Christian Primer (Third Edition),* (New York: Orbis Books, 2019), 83.

[6] J. Milburn Thompson, 84.

[7] Ibid., 87.

[8] Ibid., 85-86.

[9] Ibid., 86.

[10] https://www.c2es.org/content/ipcc-fifth-assessment-report/, accessed on 20 Jan 2020

[11] https://www.c2es.org/content/ipcc-fifth-assessment-report/, accessed on 20 Jan 2020.

[12] https://openknowledge.worldbank.org/bitstream/handle/10986/28723/9781464811555.pdf?sequence=5&isAllowed=y, accessed on 20 Jan 2020.

[13] Ibid.,

[14] https://environmentalmigration.iom.int/ipcc%E2%80%99s-fifth-assessment-report-what%E2%80%99s-it-south-asia, accessed on 10 Jan 2020.

[15] https://thediplomat.com/2019/11/climate-change-and-south-asias-pending-food-crisis/, Accessed on 10 Jan 2020.

[16] https://www.eastasiaforum.org/2018/06/17/a-storm-of-climate-change-migration-is-brewing-in-south-asia/, accessed on 12 Jan 2020.

[17] http://climatesouthasia.org/climate-change-aggravating-pakistans-water-crisis/, accessed on 10 April 2020

[18] http://climatesouthasia.org/saving-livelihoods-shadow-bagrote-valleys-melting-glaciers/, accessed on 10 April 2020.

[19] http://climatesouthasia.org/paradise-lost-maldives-climate-change/, accessed on 10 April 2020.

[20] http://climatesouthasia.org/glacier-environment-climate-change-bhutan-overview-2/, accessed on 10 April 2020.

[21] https://www.climatelinks.org/resources/sri-lanka-climate-risk-profile, accessed on 10 April 2020.

[22] https://www.climatelinks.org/resources/sri-lanka-climate-risk-profile, accessed on 10 April 2020.

[23] https://www.acclimatise.uk.com/2019/09/03/from-droughts-to-floods-the-cost-of-climate-change-for-india-continues-to-mount/, accessed on 10 March 2020.

[24] Ibid.

[25] https://qz.com/india/1806064/india-vulnerable-as-climate-refugees-surge-amid-floods-droughts/, accessed on 10 March 2020.

[26] https://qz.com/india/1806064/india-vulnerable-as-climate-refugees-surge-amid-floods-droughts/, accessed on 10 March 2020.

Chapter 2

Bible and Climate Change

Christian tradition has always considered the Bible as God's Word which informs and directs people to live according to God's will and purpose. As such, many people have misused or rather abused the Bible to deny climate change as a religious and a sociopolitical issue or to emphasise that climate change is a testament of God's wrath. However, we find that the Bible is replete with references to nature, protection of land and people, and justice to the vulnerable creatures on earth. This chapter aims to reclaim and affirm the great ecological resources available in the Bible that will help address climate change.

Climate-Deniers and the Bible

Many Christians who read the Bible in a literal sense believe that God has ordained humans to have dominion over the earth. It stems from a rather flawed interpretation of biblical verses like, "Let us make humankind in our image, according to Our likeness; and let them have dominion over the fish of the sea, and over the birds of the air, and over the cattle, and over all the wild animals of the earth, and over every creeping thing that creeps upon the earth" (Gen 1:26).

Another verse that climate-deniers use to their advantage is Psalm 8, which affirms, "God made humanity a little lower than God, had given them the right to have dominion over God's creation, putting all things under their feet. Hence the sheep and oxen, and also the beasts of the field, the birds of the air, and the fish of the sea are under the rule of the human."[1] Yet another verse that resonates with their idea of human supremacy is, "The heavens are the Lord's heavens, but the earth he has given to human beings" (Ps 115:16).

Many of them have a dislike for religious traditions that have a deep connection with nature or affirm the sacredness of nature. To buttress their point they utilise Scripture passages such as "…because they exchanged the truth about God for a lie and worshipped and served the creature rather than the Creator, who is blessed forever! Amen" (Rom 1:25).

Conservative evangelicals see environmental changes as holding a spiritual significance. According to them, plagues, earthquakes, severe floods, ecological disasters and ensuing tribulation are signs of the "end times." They decline to see the sinful greed of humans and the exploitative economic systems that cause environmental degradation and climate change. In order to substantiate their point, they quote from the Book of Revelation:

> The fourth angel poured his bowl on the sun, and it was allowed to scorch people with fire; they were scorched by the fierce heat, but they cursed the name of God, who had authority over these plagues, and they did not repent and give him glory. (Revelation 16:8-9)

With verses like this, even extreme heat conditions today is considered to be commanded by God because of human sin. Climate-deniers wilfully deny anthropogenic emissions that cause the temperature to rise and glaciers to melt. To them, human beings have nothing to do with climate change and it is something that cannot be reversed. Their claim is that nothing happens without the knowledge of God, and hence climate change and environmental disasters are part of God's plan. However, there are several passages in the Bible that prove that God cares for the earth and that human beings can participate with God in caring for God's creation which was found good by the Creator.

Old Testament: Creation Stories and the Human Role

The creation stories in the book of Genesis are ecological stories that tell us how to live realising and celebrating the plan and purpose of God the Creator along with creation. They offer spiritual and theological insights into and guidelines for reflecting on creation, ourselves and the Creator. The first chapter of Genesis narrates how God created the universe and delights in it, declaring it as "very good." The activity of the Holy Spirit begins with the creation process as "a wind from God over the face of the waters." Human beings are included in this goodness and are given the special responsibility to care for creation. More importantly, the story of Adam and Eve about humanity's fall into sin (Gen 3:1-24) is an early theological explanation of why there is suffering and evil in a world created by God of love.[2]

Several passages in the Scripture reveals how nature reflects the glory of God. Psalm 19:1 proclaims, "The heavens are telling the glory of God, and the firmament proclaims his handiwork." Job suggests that human beings look to the natural world to learn about God. "But ask the animals, they will teach you; the birds of the air, and they will tell you; ask the plants of the earth, and they will teach you; and the fish of the sea will declare to you" (Job 12:7).

Sharon Delgado, the author of *Love in a Time of Climate Change: Honoring Creation, Establishing Justice,* points out that "not all the biblical texts describe the human role as either domination or stewardship. Psalm 104 presents human beings not as masters of the created order but as members of the community of life, dependent on God's loving generosity for sustenance, as are all other beings."[3] The following scriptural passage explains God's plan for the created order, and God's commitment to renew the face of the earth:

> All creatures look to you to give them their food at the proper time. When you give it to them, they gather it up; when you open your hand, they are satisfied with good things. When you hide your face, they are terrified; when you take away their breath, they die and return to the dust. When you send your Spirit, they are created, and you renew the face of the ground. (Psalm 104: 27-28)

Even as we celebrate the above passage, it makes us remind ourselves of the damage that human beings have caused to forests, agricultural lands, waterways, coastal areas and other ecosystems, violating the integrity and beauty of God's creation. Human beings cannot praise God and at the same time destroy nature that God has created and which reflects the glory of God.

The story of Noah and the Ark is significant to understand that God's promise of protection for the future generation not only includes Noah but all creatures:

> I will remember my covenant between me and you and all living creatures of every kind. Never again will the waters become a flood to destroy all life. Whenever the rainbow appears in the clouds, I will see it and remember the everlasting covenant between God and all living creatures of every kind on the earth. So God said to Noah, "This is the sign of the covenant I have established between me and all life on the earth." (Genesis 9: 13-17)

According to Delgado, "Noah serves as a prototype for humans who seek to be faithful in protecting other species."[4] She says how saving the endangered species is a moral issue and calls such acts as a "modern-day Noah's Ark" saving as many species as possible.[5] In other words, the biblical stories invite us to rethink our attitude towards nature and take up the vocation of being Noah's Ark in the midst of erratic weather conditions.

In the context of climate crisis, it is important to know that God who created the world also set limits to it. Human beings cannot destroy it or cross the boundaries and cyclic pattern set by God. This is evident in the following texts from Isaiah:

> Who has measured the waters in the hollow of his hand, or with the breadth of his hand marked off the heavens? Who has held the dust of the earth in a basket, or weighed the mountains on the scales and the hills in a balance? (Isaiah 40:12)

> Lift up your eyes and look to the heavens: Who created all these? He who brings out the starry host one by one and calls forth each of them by name. Because of his great power and mighty strength, not one of them is missing. (Isaiah 40:26)

Frederick Quinn, a historian, points to the revelation of God in nature in the book of Isaiah. He says, "The environmental passages are not set apart like national parks; they disclose God's presence in history. These passages have a tender and redemptive quality." For instance, the following passage in Isaiah after the destruction of the Temple and the Jewish dispersion in the Babylonian community says:

> You heavens above, rain down my righteousness; let the clouds shower it down. Let the earth open wide, let salvation spring up, let righteousness flourish with it; I, the Lord, have created it. (Isaiah 45:8)

Non-human Characters in the Bible

In several stories in the Bible non-human characters become active agents of God. In his exegetical study on the book of Jonah, Raymond F. Person Jr. points out how the several non-human characters in the story—the mighty wind, the mighty storm, the sea (Jonah 1:4-15), the ship (1:4), lots (1:7), the large fish (2:1-2,11), the animals of Nineveh (3:7-8; 4:11), the *qiqayon* plant (4:6-10), the worm (4:7), the fierce east wind (4:8), and the sun (4:8)—served God's purpose.[6]

When Jonah tries to escape God's command to proclaim the word of God in Nineveh and run away, the Lord sends mighty winds towards the sea so that a mighty storm rages upon it (Jonah 1:4). It is a simple affirmation of God's partnership with God's creation to realise the divine mission of renewing the face of the earth. Jonah's assertion to the sailors that "I worship the Lord who made the sea and the dry land" (1:9) amply expresses this point.

Person also makes a marked reference to how non-human characters listen to God's commandment and act as active agents of God. The fish, the animals of Nineveh, the plant, the worm, and the wind respond to God's verbal commands. He describes it as follows: "Then the Lord spoke to the fish and it vomited Jonah upon the dry land" (Jonah 2:11). The Lord also 'appoints' the plant to give Jonah shade (4:6), the worm to kill the plant (4:7), and the wind presumably to destroy Jonah's booth (4:8); each of these characters responds obediently. With the plant and the booth no longer providing shade, 'the sun attacked Jonah's head' (4:8). That is, the sun seems to understand its role in the Lord's plan after the worm and wind have done their job."[7] What we find here is the divine affirmation of the agency of non-human beings in the divine drama of creation, sustenance and redemption.

Significantly, God shows deep compassion on human beings and for all other beings in God's creation.

> But the LORD said, "You have been concerned about this plant, though you did not tend it or make it grow. It sprang up overnight and died overnight. And should I not have concern for the great city of Nineveh, in which there are more than a hundred and twenty thousand people who cannot tell their right hand from their left—and also many animals?" (Jonah 4:10-11)

The story of Jonah is thus a pointer towards God's love and concern that transcends Israel, the chosen race, and human beings, the crown of creation, created in God's own image. According to Person, the story of Jonah teaches us to go beyond ethnocentrism and anthropocentrism and to be obedient to God's will by being more attentive to others in the earth community, including the fish, the worm, the plant, the wind, the sea and the cattle.[8]

Along with the animals, it is also important for us to have a new look at the tree, which is a dominant theme in the Bible. The tree of life is central to the garden of Eden, and the tree of life is an important image in the Book of Revelation too. Also, the tree is a recurrent motif in the prophetic books of Ezekiel and Daniel. Frederick Quinn points out that the tree has a significant aspect in biblical literature as it demonstrates God's pronouncement of suffering and redemption.[9]

The book of Ezekiel (sixth century BC) contains a messianic allegory in chapter 17:22-24:

> This is what the Sovereign LORD says: I will take a shoot from the very top of a cedar and plant it; I will break off a tender sprig from its topmost shoots and plant it on a high and lofty

> mountain. On the mountain heights of Israel, I will plant it; it will produce branches and bear fruit and become a splendid cedar. Birds of every kind will nest in it; they will find shelter in the shade of its branches. All the trees of the forest will know that I the Lord bring down the tall tree and make the low tree grow tall. I dry up the green tree and make the dry tree flourish. I the Lord have spoken, and I will do it.

Here the Messiah is compared to the branch of a cedar plant, which signifies the whole creation. The above text also allegorises the outcome of disobedience of kings to God as the destruction of the tree. This is again affirmed in Ezekiel:

> [A]nd the most ruthless of foreign nations cut it down and left it. Its boughs fell on the mountains and in all the valleys; its branches lay broken in all the ravines of the land. All the nations of the earth came out from under its shade and left it. All the birds settled on the fallen tree, and all the wild animals lived among its branches. (Ezekiel 31:12-13)

Similarly, in the book of Daniel, King Nebuchadnezzar is compared to a tree and the "holy one" demands the tree to be cut down because of his pride.

Trees are also used to signify God's redemption. Just as human sin brings about destruction and desolation of land, God's love and forgiveness is represented by green shoots. The biblical passages on the Messiah in Isaiah says, "A shoot will come up from the stump of Jesse; from his roots a branch will bear fruit" (Isa 11:1).

Again, it is said that this new tree, the Messiah, symbolises a new peaceable kingdom where the wolf will live with the lamb, the leopard with the kid, the calf and the young lion feed together and little children tend to them (Isa 11:6). Also, the wild animals, the poisonous vipers and people will live together (Isa 8:9).

Sabbath and Jubilee, Land Ethics in the Bible

The biblical concepts of Sabbath and Jubilee are about ecological justice as much as they are about social and economic justice. One of the main reasons for climate crisis is that the earth and its resources are plundered constantly for corporate greed without allowing it rest and rejuvenation.

Work and leisure, activity and rest form the natural rhythm of God's created order. Genesis 2:2-3 illustrates how God works and then rests and how the whole created order is called to repeat the experience of divine rest and rejuvenation. This rest challenges the idea that humans should constantly work for life to flourish and for which the resources of the earth should be used up completely. Rest defines the different characters of God. Anne Rowthorn puts forward the different nature of God based on the above text thus:

> God at work and God at rest; God in action, God in repose; God engaged, God at ease; God in effort, God in pause; God in creating; God in stillness; God in thunderclap, God in silence and calm. In some respects, the seventh day gives meaning to the other six, for in it we picture a resting God in Creation, a God who pauses to let the magnificence of the created order penetrate him. For six days God has worked on the natural world; now God stands aside to allow the natural world to affect him. "And God saw that it was good." It is a divine reciprocity, a divine rhythm: God acts in the first instance, and in second God is acted upon.[10]

The sabbath assumes significance in Jewish history too as a compulsory day of solemn "rest" (Exod 20:11 and 31:17). More importantly, after the exodus of the Israelites, rest was a necessary commandment in remembrance of their slavery in Egypt that denied them real rest. In Deuteronomy 5:14-15, sabbath is not only a period of rest, but also has a deeper theological significance of restoration, setting things right and as a time to readjust the order of society. The sabbath rest is not just for one day of the week but extends to the sabbatical year (one year in seven years, Lev 25:4)… and the jubilee year (Lev 25:8), the fiftieth year in which the slaves and the land are returned to their owner. This is the beautiful rhythm of God's divine design for us.

The world's people are always in stress and live without harmony because of climate crisis. The sabbath observance challenges the restless nature of humans and their fast-paced economy which destroys the peace of the earth and its inhabitants. What is needed is divine peace that restores the order of God's creation.

Gospels: Jesus and Nature

Earth and nature are persistent themes in the life and teachings of Jesus. The parables and wisdom sayings of Jesus to explain God's vision for this world show his deep understanding and close connection with the natural world. Niels Henrik Gregersen illustrates how Jesus uses examples from nature in his teachings: Jesus compares the coming of God's kingdom to the growth of a mustard seed (Matt 13.31-32); he instructs his followers to live as unworried as the birds of the air and as lilies of the field (Matt. 6 25-34); he also teaches his disciples to pray to God the Father by stretching their imagination between the high and the low: "Your will be done, on earth as it is in heaven" (Matt 6.10). The disciples, moreover, are required to become "the salt of the earth" (Matt 5.13). Also, speaking to those who were not part of the inner circle of disciples, Jesus says, "Blessed are the meek, for they will inherit the earth" (Matt 5.5).[11]

Several passages in the Gospels say how Jesus spent time "outside" in prayer (Mark 6:46). Other stories also emphasise

Jesus' power over nature, demonstrating the power of God of creation working through him.[12] When Jesus was tempted he was with the wild beasts (Mark 1:13). When the disciples feared that they would drown, Jesus stilled the storm (Mark 4:35-41). He walked on water (Mark 6:47-51).

Sharon Delgado speaks of the many times Jesus used metaphors and parables relating to the natural world, which were very familiar to his listeners who lived in an agrarian culture. The parables of the sower (Matt 13:1-23), the mustard seed (Matt 13:30-32), the weeds among the wheat (Matt 13:36-43) and the lost sheep (Luke 15: 1-7) not only imparted spiritual lessons to his followers but affirmed their role as caretakers of creation.[13]

For discerning the times Jesus pointed to the created world. When he says, "The birds have nests but also falls down from the sky, yet no sparrow will fall to the ground apart from the Father's will" (Matt 10.29), he teaches that God has a pattern for the created world and is in control of it. In another place Jesus says we have to *learn* to live like the sparrows or the ravens (Luke 12.24).

Gregersen says Jesus even compares the human art of weather forecasting to the need for self-knowledge and of interpreting the signs of their times and circumstances:

> When you see a cloud rising in the west, you immediately say, "It is going to rain"; and so it happens. And when you see the south wind blowing, you say, "There will be scorching heat"; and it happens. You hypocrites! You know how to interpret the appearance of the earth and sky, but why do you not know how to interpret the present time? (Luke 12: 54-57)

Delgado interprets the parable of the wicked tenant (Matt 21:33-46) to mean human beings' sin of refusal to care for the earth's gift on behalf of God. According to her, Jesus uses the image of the tenant gardeners to represent the human race. Now, these wicked tenants not only refuse to give the owner a share of the harvest, but they also reject the owner's servants and finally kill his son.[14] We see here the connection between violence against earth and violence against nature.

Jesus' teaching on futuristic judgments also poses questions on how we think about the well-being of our future generations. Gregersen shows how the parable of the Son of Man coming in glory to judge all people (Matt. 25. 31-46) raises the question of the needy and thirsty in our times. Those in need could be the non-human species and people who are the victims of climate change. The parable of the judgment clearly asserts how the Son of Man has established kinship relations beyond genetic divides to anyone needy, thirsty and hungry and anyone who could be the victims of ecological disasters and climate change.[15]

Earth's Cry and Apocalyptic Texts

Several biblical passages talk about the mourning and groaning of creation. These point to the earth's pain and the yearning for God's liberation. They also can be seen as a public witness of creation welcoming an ethical vision for the entire world to change.

One of the very prominent texts is from Hosea:

> Hear the word of the Lord, you Israelites, because the Lord has a charge to bring against you who live in the land: "There is no faithfulness, no love, no acknowledgment of God in the land. There is only cursing, lying and murder, stealing and adultery; they break all bounds, and bloodshed follows bloodshed. Because of this the land dries up, and all who live in it waste away; the beasts of the field, the birds in the sky and the fish in the sea are swept away. (Hosea 4:1-3)

The earth is an active agent through which Yahweh's judgment is rendered. It is interesting to note how the earth and the entire cosmos is governed not only by physical laws but also by the moral order of Yahweh. Melissa Tubbs Loya points out how the mourning, languishing, and perishing of the earth and its inhabitants described by Hosea are consequences of Israel's breach of this moral order through the crimes they commit against each other.[16]

Here, Hosea points out that the earth's mourning will affect "all who live in it" and also the animals of the field, the birds of the air, and the fish of the sea. The sins of Israel affect the earth and all creatures in it. According to Loya, this mourning is a call for humans to move away from anthropocentric approaches to living and to come back to God's created order.[17]

Earth's lament and the call for humans to mourn and repent for their sins occur again in the book of Joel:

> A nation has invaded my land, a mighty army without number; it has the teeth of a lion, the fangs of a lioness. It has laid waste my vines and ruined my fig trees. It has stripped off their bark and thrown it away, leaving their branches white. Mourn like a virgin in sackcloth grieving for the betrothed of her youth. Grain offerings and drink offerings are cut off from the house of the Lord. The priests are in mourning, those who minister before the Lord. The fields are ruined, the ground is dried up; the grain is destroyed, the new wine is dried up, the olive oil fails. (Joel 1:6-10)

Laurie J. Braaten points out that God's lament here includes "my land! my vines! and my fig trees!" and it is part of the lament "Alas my daughter! or Alas my brother" in the previous verses. God's lament also expresses the pain and pathos about "the fields being dried up" and "the grain being destroyed." Verses 13-14 are a call for the priests to lament the loss of the grain and drink offerings and for all the inhabitants to fast and cry out to God.

The lament continues in the following verses, with even animals moaning in hunger and herds of cattle wandering about confused because they have no pasture. The flocks of sheep and goats bleat in misery (verse 18). Of special significance are verses 19-20:

> To you, Lord, I call, for fire has devoured the pastures in the wilderness and flames have burned up all the trees of the field. Even the wild animals pant for you; the streams of water have dried up and fire has devoured the pastures in the wilderness. (Joel 19-20)

Here, Braaten says that the voice "upon you, Oh YHWH, I call!" is the community's lament and call to God. But which is this community? To this question, Braaten says that the most appropriate speaker here is the earth. That the earth is appealing to God for deliverance is explicitly articulated in this verse.[18]

The earth's call here is to challenge human beings and bring into their consciousness the consequences of sin and what humans should do to correct it. A similar idea is seen in the words of Prophet Jeremiah:

> Many shepherds will ruin my vineyard and trample down my field; they will turn my pleasant field into a desolate wasteland. It will be made a wasteland, parched and desolate before me; the whole land will be laid waste because there is no one who cares. (Jeremiah 12:10-11)

The verse "because there is no one who cares" (verse 11) signifies the nonchalant attitude of humans even after witnessing the earth's destruction.

The book of Joel affirms how the present-day climate and ecological crisis exemplifies earth's mourning. It is also a call for humans to identify with the earth's suffering. "Earth also condemns human's sin; Earth's suffering stands as a sign to humans that they have not repented of the damage they have done to the Earth."[19]

A prominent text about the groaning of the creation in the New Testament is from Paul's letter to the Romans.

> I consider that our present sufferings are not worth comparing with the glory that will be revealed in us. For the creation waits in eager expectation for the children of God to be revealed. For the creation was subjected to frustration, not by its own choice, but by the will of the one who subjected it, in hope that the creation itself will be liberated from its bondage to decay and brought into the freedom and glory of the children of God. We know that the whole creation has been groaning as in the pains of childbirth right up to the present time. Not only so, but we ourselves, who have the first fruits of the Spirit, groan inwardly as we wait eagerly for our adoption to sonship, the redemption of our bodies. For in this hope we were saved. But hope that is seen is no hope at all. Who hopes for what they already have? But if we hope for what we do not yet have, we wait for it patiently. In the same way, the Spirit helps us in our weakness. We do not know what we ought to pray for, but the Spirit himself intercedes for us through wordless groans. (Romans 8:18-26)

Delgado invokes the Wesleyan tradition of social holiness to reflect on God's universal love and the deliverance extended to all creation. In one of his famous sermons "The General Deliverance," based on Romans 8, John Wesley refers to the cry of the creation caused by human sin.[20] This Romans text assures us that one day the human and the created order will attain redemption from this groaning. The key here for the redemption and the renewal of the earth is that humans need to repent and return to their right relationship with God and the created order.[21]

The present climate crisis has created a hopeless situation. We are challenged to envision hope in the present scenario. The Romans text invites us to envision hope even amid this severe climate crisis. Delgado describes this aspect in times of climate change as follows:

> It is not easy to be hopeful when considering the accelerating release of greenhouse gases, rising global temperatures, and ever-increasing weather-related disasters. Creation's groaning is starting to sound more like death groans than labor pains. Yet this text invites us to trust that God intends for new life to be born out of creation's current travail. There is still hope that human beings will live in right relationship with God, with each other and with creation. To commit oneself to this hopeful vision is an audacious leap of faith, an act of hope that itself engenders new life.[22]

Thus, the cry of the earth in the Scripture is not merely about fear or hopelessness in our lives but is an invitation to be present in the midst of these crises and realise that God is present in the crises. This will help us reimagine a new future along with God, the earth and all its inhabitants.

Apocalyptic books in the Bible offer a lot to interpret the socio-economic reasons for climate change. They also help in giving moral courage to pronounce the end of empires that destruct the earth and also in assuring a promise of God's renewal of this earth. T.J. Gorringe shows how the Book of Revelation is an important text to address climate change. He cites three important reasons for using Revelation as follows:[23]

> First of all, it is what we call 'apocalyptic' literature. Apocalypse does not mean catastrophe and disaster, as we tend to use the word. It means disclosing, exposing, making manifest, holding up this world to the judgment of God. It has nothing to do with 'the end of the world' or its 'extermination'. As [Jurgen] Moltmann puts it: 'What Jewish and Christian apocalyptic intends is not to

evoke horror in the face of the end, but to encourage endurance in resistance to the powers of this world.' That is the first key reason for going to Revelation.

Second, apocalyptic literature is basically an underground literature, communicating in a symbolic language. Symbols run deeper than words and the symbols from this particular book have done much to shape the Western imagination. Unfortunately, our own rational mindset makes little of them.

Third, the book of Revelation is a patchwork of quotations from the Hebrew Bible, and perhaps includes, as we shall see, echoes of what we now know as Synoptic material. The author is scripturally literate…. The book of Revelation, therefore, encourages us in scriptural literacy.

Revelation 8:6-12 denotes the blowing of trumpets by the angels as destruction that falls on the earth (verse 7), the sea (verse 8), the rivers (verse 10) and heaven/sky (verse 12). This is very similar to the blowing of trumpets by the prophets in the Old Testament as a sign of God's warning.

In the context of climate change, the blowing of trumpet is a call for repentance to change our lifestyle.[24] Gorringe points to scientific facts of climate change as trumpets that are already blowing. The increase in CO_2 levels, the Arctic ocean losing its 40 per cent volume of ice sheets, two-thirds of South Asia's disasters being climate-related, the unpredictability of extreme weather patterns, etc., are the trumpet sounds now.[25] The Book of Revelation calls the church to "wake up." The call to repentance is a call to action and a call to reshape our economy and our ways of living.

"John's vision of God" in Revelation captures a different reality other than the power of Rome. Says Gorringe: "There is a throne in heaven, there is an alternative power at work in history. It is the power of love—as the vision of the Lamb will reveal—a power which aims at redeeming life and sustaining it."[26] This also reminds us that there is an alternative world possible.

The Book of Revelation is not God's vengeance story; rather, it is God's pronouncement of justice against the empire and its system destroying the world which is manifested as climate change today. This is a story of God's redeeming act of the human and the non-human world which is caught in the midst of destructive forces, causing climate change. Books like Revelation invite us to be aware of the climate crisis, encourage us to challenge the forces causing it, and to envision hope and life in the midst of catastrophes because the God of love still loves this world.

Thus, the Bible is a great resource for our faithful engagement in the world in addressing ecological disasters and climate change. The rich ecological themes in the Bible prove that God has always been expressing God's ways, be it spiritual or ethical, through nature. Reading the Bible with fresh eyes from the perspective of the earth in the context of climate change will allow us to experience that God still speaks to us through the created world and invites us to learn from it and work along with the natural world to establish God's reign.

Endnotes

[1] https://journals.sagepub.com/doi/pdf/10.1177/0096340215599789, accessed on 9 Feb 2020.

[2] Sharon Delgado, *Love in a Time of Climate Change: Honoring Creation, Establishing Justice,* (Minneapolis: Fortress Press, 2017), 44.

[3] Ibid., 45-46.

[4] Ibid., 46.

[5] Ibid., 46.

[6] Raymond F. Person Jr. "The Role of Nonhuman Characters in Jonah," in *Exploring Ecological Hermeneutics* edited by Norman C. Habel and Peter Trudinger (Atlanta: Society of Biblical Literature, 2008), 85.

[7] Ibid., 86-87.

[8] Ibid., 90.

[9] Frederick Quinn, *To Heal the Earth: A Theology of Ecology*, (Nashville: Upper Room Books, 1994), 43.

[10] Anne Rowthorn, *Caring for Creation*, (Wilton: Morehouse Publishing,1989), 42-43.

[11] Niels Henrik Gregerseon, 42

[12] Sharon Delgado, 47.

[13] Ibid., 47.

[14] Ibid., 47.

[15] Niels Henrik Gregersen, 46.

[16] Melissa Tubbs Loya, "Therefore the Earth Mourns": The Grievance of Earth in Hosea 4:1-3," in *Exploring Ecological Hermeneutics* edited by Norman C. Habel and Peter Trudinger (Atlanta: Society of Biblical Literature, 2008), 54.

[17] Ibid., 62.

[18] Ibid., 67.

[19] Ibid., 69.

[20] http://wesley.nnu.edu/john-wesley/the-sermons-of-john-wesley-1872-edition/sermon-60-the-general-deliverance/, accessed on 10 Feb 2020.

[21] Sharon Delgado, 51.

[22] Ibid., 54.

[23] http://operationnoah.org/wp-content/uploads/2014/06/Theology-Visions-of-the-end-pdf.pdf,

[24] T.J. Gorringe takes this quotation from the commentary of Bas Wielenga, *Revelation to John: Tuning into Songs of Moses and the Lamb*, New Delhi: ISPCK 2009, 63.

[25] Ibid.,

[26] Ibid.,

Chapter 3

Climate Change and Christian Faith

Climate change is not just an environmental issue but is a profound theological problem as well. There is a tendency to say that Christian theology and doctrines have nothing to do with climate change. However, in the face of climate change, Christian faith articulation has a great role in restoring and preserving God's creation. For those of us who revision church as an event that happens in the life of our communities, helping life to flourish, climate change ought to be a faith issue.

This particular section addresses climate change through basic Christian theology and doctrines, asking questions such as "Where is God?" and "What is the human role?" in mitigating the climate crisis. It also delves on issues such as sin and the work of the Holy Spirit in revisioning salvation.

God's Presence in this World: Incarnation and Trinity

The dominant thinking throughout the ages whenever a weather-related disaster occurred was to consider it as an act of God, or rather wrath of God, for human sin. The general belief was and is that God punishes human beings using nature. This has led to several false assumptions about the understanding of God and God's role in terms of climate change. This is partly also because of theological perceptions about a transcendent, unchanging, all-powerful God who is above earthly realities. This view holds that only human beings are destined to benefit from God's grace and that climate change and ecological concerns are not spiritual matters.[1]

But there are also people who believe that God is always present not only to sustain human life but to sustain the whole of this created world. The theological understanding of "the world as the body of God" and of the "Trinitarian God" affirm that God is ever present and working towards the redemption of the earth and humanity. Sallie Mcfague derives from Ramanuja a wonderful concept called "The world as God's body." She says that "if God is always incarnate, if God is always in us and we in God," then an appropriate model to understand God is to consider the world as God's body.[2] Hence, for Christians, the doctrine of creation and the doctrine of incarnation cannot be seen differently. God, who created us and in whom we live and exist, is not apart from this world. There is always continuity between God and this world.

McFague says the very idea of God taking flesh in Jesus Christ is appropriate for interpreting the Christian doctrine of creation in the time of climate change. This is better understood by the theological understanding of the world as God's body, which predicates that the doctrine of creation is not primarily about God's power but also about God's love and how we can all live together within and for God's body. Here we meet God in the world in the hungry, the sick and, now, also in the victims of climate change. This incarnation theology strongly affirms that loving the earth and taking care of God's creation is an important Christian vocation in this time of climate crisis.[3]

The above model has three implications. One, it challenges us to know about this world and how it functions as an "ecological unity" in order to understand its complexity and to celebrate its diversity. Further, this model affirms that God is ever present in this world and that human beings are called to be partners with God in maintaining the health of all creation. Here human beings cannot simply consider themselves as the crown of creation but as part of creation and who are at the same time the neediest of all creatures and the most powerful.[4]

The second implication is that if the world is God's body "then God is the source, the centre, the spring, the spirit of all that lives and loves, all that is beautiful and true."[5] It affirms that the universe becomes God's body, God's glory, and a sacrament of God's presence with us. We depend totally on the gifts of God's body—air, food, water, land, and other creatures. We cannot escape from God's presence. God whom we meet through the earth is the source not only of "my being but of all beings." Hence, though as human beings we acknowledge our mistake for our responsibility for climate change, we do not face this overwhelming problem on our own. God is with us as the source and power of all our efforts to live differently.[6]

The third implication of this model, according to McFague, is that God is *in charge* but does not want to control all the events; rather, God wants human beings to be God's partner. As we totally trust in God it also pushes us to get involved with our neighbours to see how we can live justly and sustainably.[7]

Hence this model emphasises that God is always incarnated, and creation is the witness of that continuous presence with us.

But God wants us and nature to work together to live in this reality and bring in change for a peaceful coexistence.

Trinitarian Theology

The Triune God is an important theological doctrine for Christians. Right from the early days of the church, Christians have found themselves praying to God the Father, through the Son, in the Spirit. Timothy Gorringe says that the Trinity implies not only a "spiritual Trinity" but also a "social Trinity," implying how we should live in this world. This bears on our understanding of society, economy and climate change.[8] This relational aspect of Trinity invites us not only to understand God who exists in loving relation within the three forms but also implies our ethical relationship to God and to one another. This relational aspect of Trinity also teaches us that this biological, chemical and physical world is all relational and that human beings are totally in a *relational* interdependence with the world that God has created. When the church confesses its faith in the triune God, it is a belief in a God who seeks communion and an intimate relationship with creation. This strongly implies that redemption is not apart from this created world. Karen Bloomquist asserts this as she says, "Creation is far more than just a backdrop for God's main redemptive activity in human history. It is the redemption of *all* creation that is at stake (Rom 8), not redemption *from* creation."[9]

This relational and redemptive aspect of Trinity, which reminds us that this world is in a mutually loving relationship, is significant in terms of climate change because it urges us to be concerned about our carbon emissions that would affect people who live in a different and distant place. Further, the aspect of Trinity also challenges the fixed norms created by the capitalist economy where only money and wealth decides everything, and invites us into a relational indwelling cutting across differences and boundaries to experience life in an intimate relationship with the marginalised and vulnerable communities.

Metropolitan Paulos Mar Gregorios, one of the pioneer Orthodox ecotheologians in India, puts forward an integral theology based on the biblical doctrine of creation and the Eastern Orthodox theology of Trinity, developing his idea from the classical cosmology of Gregory of Nyssa. According to his explanation, Trinitarian theology is an integral theology where the three divine natures of God are in a relationship called *perichoresis*.[10] It is an integral relationship that affirms the conditions of wholeness, responsivity, mutuality and mystery.[11] This integral theology affirms that the Creator and the creation are not separate, and in their organic unity they experience and celebrate their mutual flourishing.[12]

Ecological Anthropology: Human Responsibility in this World

Anthropology is the study of human beings, societies, cultures and their civilisational developments. Ecological anthropology forms a subfield aiming to understand the complex relationship between people and their environment. What climate change has exposed is human exploitation of the created order. At the heart of capitalism is the view that the earth's resources do not have any intrinsic value except to serve human beings. Traditional Christian belief has also promoted that human beings are the crown of creation. Ecological degradation and climate change has prompted Christian theology to deconstruct its anthropocentric (human-centred) approaches to life.

Sallie McFague says a "turn away from anthropocentrism—the focus on ourselves as masters of the earth—to cosmocentrism, the focus on earth and where we belong in it"[13] will help all of us to live justly and sustainably on our home, planet earth. The human role is to realise that we are related to everything else and our response ought to be *appreciation* and *care.* [14]

She invites us to see ourselves as part of the web of life, an incredibly vast, complex, subtle, beautiful web that would amaze us and bring forth our concerns. We need to see the earth as our home. Using this home metaphor, she tells us to 1) take only your share; 2) clean up after yourself; and 3) keep the house in good repair for others.[15]

According to McFague, "ecological anthropology is neither an esoteric knowledge for specialists nor a sentimental plea to 'love nature.' Rather, it is *the truth about who we are*—the best truth, at least, that we presently have. It tells us where we fit in the scheme of things…. It reminds us that instead of being the center of creation, we are from moment to moment depending on all that is, so to speak, 'beneath us' (all of the animate and inanimate energy sources)."[16] It is a call to see how we can become God's helpers and avoid the destruction of the earth.

As mentioned earlier, a great misperception prevails among Christians on the idea of "dominion" in the Genesis story (Gen 1: 28). Who gave humans dominion? Has God really given humans the power to establish control over the rest of creation, as the term implies? In order to understand this, we need to have a clear understanding of the God-given responsibility for us in this world. Paulos Mar Gregorios, in his book *The Human Presence: Ecological Spirituality and the Age of the Spirit,* emphasises the mediatory and participatory role of humanity in relation to God and the world. According to him, humans have a vocation as "priests of creation." The priest should radiate grace and glory from God to creation and offer creation to God through self-offering.

Larry Rasmussen develops four ways to understand the role of humans in relation to creation: *Steward, Partner, Sacrament/ Priest,* and *Prophet/Covenant.*

Steward: The Hebrew verse *l' ovdah ul' shomrah* ("to till and keep" of Gen 2:15) literally means "to serve and preserve." Here, Rasmussen points out that "to serve means, literally, to cultivate," and the word steward (*shomrei*) simply means guardian, custodian, and preserver of the earth.[17] The source of their being and purpose of Adam and Eve can be explained only with respect to their intimate relationship with the earth. Adam is derived from *Adama,* the Hebrew word for topsoil, earth or ground, and Eve, or *Hava,* literally means living. Hence, together Adam and Eve signify "Soil and Life."[18]

According to the Jewish rabbinical tradition, the significance of the sabbath is to restore this primordial and proper relationship of humans with the rest of nature. No way does it mean dominion.

Partner: This model clearly affirms how human beings are not the centre of creation (homocentrism) and calls for human beings to understand the interconnectedness and interdependence of all things on which humans exercise their power.[19] Here human beings are called to partner with nature and to work in participation with the earth's inhabitants and not in their own selfish ways.

Sacrament/Priest: Rasmussen derives the idea of human as sacrament/priest from the Orthodox tradition. It is understood to mean that as priests, humans can represent creation and give voice to it in the cosmic liturgy of praise; we are the mediators, not the centre, and we intercede for the community of life and speak on its behalf before God. Rasmussen says, "We are *imago mundi* (image of the world) who, as also *imago Dei* (image of God), voice God to creation and creation to God."[20] By lifting up creation as a sacrament and considering the earth as holy is not to say that it *is* God. Rather, it is *of* God; God is present in its presence. This is an important distinction we need to recognise. The foundational belief of Christianity is panentheism (it is *of* God) and not pantheism (it *is* God). Hence, when human beings participate in a sacramental and priestly role, they are called to mainly uphold their moral role towards creation. It challenges the human nature to master, control and distance themselves from creation but invites them to be present, have a relationship, and give care and respect due to the sacred.[21]

Prophet/Covenant: The covenant model basically speaks about the need to adhere to covenantal terms. The covenant here refers to God's covenant to Noah in Genesis 9:12-13: "God said, 'This is the sign of covenant that I make between me and you and every living creature that is with you, for all future generation: I have set the bow in my clouds, and it shall be a sign of the covenant between me and the earth." Any injustice done to the land and its people is a violation of the covenant. To keep the covenant is to maintain peace with one another and with the land. The breaking of the covenant involves injustice to the land and its people. The role of the prophet here is to remind human beings when they transgress the covenantal terms. Based on this, Rasmussen suggests that the need for today is ecoprophetism, which invokes "the moral call to strike the religious consciousness of the people."[22]

In this context, he also explains that *imago Dei* (image of God) simply means that we reflect the purpose of God in us to live peacefully and contribute to the purpose of God's creation in this world. It is mirroring God's way in this world. "Imaging God is acting in a godly way toward one another and other creatures. Imaging God is loving earth fiercely, as God does."[23] Imaging God is being the prophet of God in this world.

Humans as Relational Beings Defined by the Ethics of Love

Cynthia Moe-Lobeda points out the emergence of relational theologies which emphasise that human beings are ontologically relational. This means we are created to be in relation with others. According to her, "we are called to receive the love of God and live it into the world."[24] That is, we are relational creatures and because of our practical responsibilities we are also political creatures and at the same time we are also earth creatures.[25]

Moe-Lobeda points out how Irenaeus of Lyons (second-century theologian) calls us "mud creatures," which is derived from the Hebrew word *ha adam*—crafted from Adama (dust of the earth, topsoil). She goes on to further explain scientifically that humans are made from *humus* and we are part of the animal kingdom, the phylum *Chordata*, the genus *Homo*, and the species *Homo sapiens*. At this point our God-given task as mud creatures is to analyse our relationship with the rest of nature and creation and to re-see and re-situate ourselves *within*, rather than above, earth's web of life.[26]

From the perspective of the ethic of love and a theological and biological perspective, Moe-Lobeda offers a detailed definition of human beings and their role which can be summarised as follows: As "mud creatures" human beings are an utterly dependent species on earth. We share our origins with the earth community and hence also our salvation. We live within a *polis* and *economia* with the planet. We are mainly called to express God's love in this world and to commit ourselves to work with everybody to make this world more sustainable and just.[27]

Ecological Christology

Ecological Christology is the study of how the life and ministry of Jesus Christ is relevant to the present context of ecological disasters and climate change. It is important to recognise that Jesus' life and ministry are not a foregone historical reality; Jesus is present in today's world inspiring us to carry out his mission of teaching, healing and prophesying to establish the reign of God in this world. That Jesus Christ continues to reveal and reidentify with the material realities of our life. The verse "He himself is before all things, and in him all things hold together" (Col 1.17)[28] makes this plain. Jesus is an ever-present reality in the crisis of climate change. N.H. Gregersen captures it beautifully as follows:

> The Son of God, who is eternally born out of the Father, is present as the incarnate Jesus Christ, forever living with and for all other creatures in the universal through the working of the Holy Spirit. Jesus Christ is thus not a bygone historical individual, on whom we can look back in historical distance, but synchronous with each creature in time and co-inherent in all that exists in time and space.[29]

The life of Jesus, his teachings, the genealogical records in the Gospels, his table fellowship with the neglected in society all prove that Jesus has a biological body and a social body. At the same time, he always represents people to God and represents the values of God (whom he called *Abba*) to this world. Jesus was and is still concerned about this world. In his birth, Jesus

Christ is called Immanuel (God with us) and the resurrected Jesus returned to be "among" his disciples (Luke 24:36).[30]

Gregersen says that "the earth is a recurrent motif in the teaching of Jesus. There seems to be a strong affinity between God's 'inner' nature and God's external work in creation."[31] When Jesus referred to himself as the Son of Man it was his affirmation that he wanted to identify with the earth. Son of Man in Aramaic is *bar anash,* corresponding to *ben adam* in Hebrew, which means 'son of Adam'; in that sense Jesus was the son of the son of the earth.

The word (logos) becoming flesh (*sarx*) is also an important concept in making relevant Jesus' incarnation in the context of climate change. This idea of God becoming flesh in this world expresses how God loves this world in its biological and sociological existence. Gregersen says: "Divinity does not hide *behind* the flesh, neither did he appear only in the flesh in a transitory manner. Rather, the divine Logos genuinely 'became flesh' (*sarx geneto*) and was present in Jesus as flesh, *with* the flesh of others, and *for* all flesh."[32] This divine logos encompasses the entire realm of humanity—earth, creatures and the soil. Thus 'word becoming flesh' in Jesus means that God is ever present in the biological and social reality and also wants to *save* humanity and this world from degradation.

Apart from the incarnation of Christ, the cross and the resurrection give Christians a strong moral power to participate actively in changing this world. Moe-Lobeda says that the cross exposes the human sin of being selfish and at the same time it opens our eyes to see that we cannot exclude ourselves from the reality of systemic sin.[33] In the context of climate change, the cross enables us to see our sins against the earth and unleashes the moral power to be disciples of Christ in resisting the political and economic structures that destroy this earth.

The story of the cross ends in the resurrection. While the cross exposes our sin and gives the moral power to act, the resurrection gives us great hope that the present climate crisis can change. This hope is important in the context of several ecological devastations rendering many communities hopeless. Here the cross and the resurrection give great courage and hope to face climate crisis. Moe-Lobeda explains this power of hope in the cross and the resurrection as follows:

> The power of God liberating all of creation from the bonds of oppression, destruction and death is stronger than all that would undermine God's promise of abundant life for all. A soul searing, life-shattering destruction and death are not the last words; the end of the story is resurrection. The last word is life raised out of brutal death. In the midst of suffering and death—whether individual, social, or ecological—the promise given to the earth community is that life in God will reign.[34]

Finally, Moe-Lobeda, from a Lutheran perspective, affirms, "Everything is full of Christ…. Christ fills all things…. Christ is around us, in us and in all places…. He is present in all creatures and I might find him in stone, in fire, in water."[35] If Christ is present in all earth's creatures and elements, then any destruction caused to the earth is crucifying Christ out of human greed and ignorance.

Hence the cross, the resurrection and the presence of Christ in all creation give us the moral courage to challenge the forces that cause climate change, protect the victims of climate change and also help us to envision a new world order.

Holy Spirit: The Moral-Spiritual Power

Christian Scripture and tradition consider the Holy Spirit as the empowering aspect of God for human beings to participate in God's healing and liberating engagement with the world. Most importantly, Christian theology affirms that the Spirit is the ongoing creative presence of God which sustains all the created beings of this world. Verses that put forward the idea include, "The spirit of God was moving over the water" (Gen 1:2); "when you send forth your spirit, they are created; and you renew the *face of the ground*" (Ps 104:30); and "In the Spirit, we live and move and have our being" (Acts 17:28).

Samuel Rayan, an Indian Jesuit theologian, in his article titled "The Earth is the Lord's," offers a biblical interpretation of the Holy Spirit from an ecological perspective. This article focuses on celebrating creation, expresses concern for its welfare, and ends by urging us to listen to nature: The earth speaks to us in "the eloquent silence of hills and trees… in the quiet language of many colours, and of graceful movements.…"[36] For him, the earth is a theological and liturgical reality because it is imbued with the Holy Spirit. He describes the integrity of creation in terms of the verses in Romans Chapter 8, which says creation itself will be liberated from its bondage to decay and brought into the freedom and glory of the children of God by the power of the Holy Spirit. The Spirit works to create mutual awareness and therefore holds the universe together. Rayan's ecotheology is perhaps best described as a "pneumatological cosmism." [37]

Kirsteen Kim points out that Rayan's concern for bread and breath in India portrays his ecotheology not simply as an aesthetic approach but also as having a deep concern for humanity.[38] Rayan strongly opposes private ownership of land and argues for a peaceful reallocation of land to people. He finds John V. Taylos' description of the Holy Spirit as the "go-between God" helpful in explaining how the Spirit works to create mutual awareness.[39]

Today people believe that they do not have an empowering source to address climate change and to understand the pains of the victims of climate change. Moe-Lobeda asserts that the Holy Spirit can help us to come out of this moral oblivion and also empower us to change our ways of living to prevent climate crisis. She points out that climate change results in a moral crisis that it is often not realised that the people who suffer acutely from climate change are also those least responsible for it; that climate privileged communities may respond to climate crisis through policies and practices but may ignore people who are the most climate vulnerable; and that sometimes, the efforts to reduce carbon emission may also endanger climate vulnerable sectors.[40]

The *Ruach,* which refers to God's spirit, is the breath of life, the animating force, in the Old Testament. This *Ruach* imbues one with discernment. Moe-Lobeda points out that "according to the Hebrew Scriptures, the spirit of God is the force of God emanating from God that enables people to act or that acts in people. It is this dimension of God that reaches into the depth of the person or the people and awakens agency or is agency for being and doing what is pleasing to God."[41]

In the New Testament, we see how the *Pneuma,* the spirit of God, anoints Jesus and gives him immense power in the face of temptation for proclaiming the reign of God and for his liberating and healing mission. Jesus also says that God will send the Spirit to be with the disciples (John 14-16), which is the spirit of truth (14:17), which shall abide in them (14:17), and teach them everything and remind them of all that Jesus taught them (14:26). After Jesus' ascension, the apostles and the people who were converted received the Holy Spirit (Acts 2:38).[42]

Moe-Lobeda says there are three ways by which we might be led by God's "spirit of truth" to negate moral oblivion and cultivate moral vision as a spiritual practice. The first is seeing "what is going on." This would mean to recognise the causal links between our lives and the destruction of the earth and communities that live close to nature. The second is seeing "What could and should be"—this pertains to just and ecologically sound ways of living practices, policies and worldviews. The third is a way of seeing that we, human beings, are not alone in the quest for a more just and sustainable way of living. The sacred life-giving, life-saving source of the cosmos—the Spirit—is with and within earth's elements and creatures, luring creation towards God's intent that all may have life and have it abundantly (John 10:10). The Spirit here enables life and love to reign over death and destruction.[43]

The Spirit's empowerment is a community event. It calls for union and communion. It challenges privatised and individual modes of living and calls for a community-oriented living. Moe-Lobeda says the Spirit may be calling forth the God-given communion that already exists but we only glimpse dimly, and it is time for us to recognise it completely and commit ourselves to change the world.[44]

Sin: Structural Violence

Sin has been understood in different ways in Christian tradition and history. Basically, sins are considered as personal or individual. In a much deeper sense, it is turning away from God and focusing more on oneself.

In the context of climate change, it is important to perceive sin as functioning in socio-economic structural relationships that affect societies and create a great impact on ecosystems. Moe-Lobeda says one has to seriously look into the structural aspects of sin in the context of climate change. According to her, "the increasing destructive power of humankind, seen most blatantly in the build-up of nuclear weaponry and destructive climate change, calls for probing structural sin and its power more deeply."[45]

Hence sin, which is the attitude of "selves curved in on self," expands to not only individuals and societies but to all of humankind's relationship with the rest of creation. Sin here is a disoriented relationship with God, self, others, and "the rest of creation."[46] While personal sins such as over-consumption and self-interest are significant in this context, climate change speaks more about structural sin or social sin rooted in the profit-oriented market economy manifested in the form of over-emitting industrial developments.

According to Moe-Lobeda, there are four defining features of structural injustice as structural sin: 1) The relative invisibility of structural injustice to those who do not suffer directly from it; 2) the fact that structural injustice continues regardless of the virtue or vice of people involved; 3) its transmission from generation to generation unless exposed and confronted; and 4) its expansion as a result of concentrated power.[47]

In the context of socioecological injustice, structural sin is the lack of awareness about communities that are affected due to climate change, over-consumption for several generations by the rich and the affluent, and our failure to challenge ecologically unjust economic practices. Renouncing this structural sin to create a moral-spiritual awakening for collective effort and action is the need of the hour.

Salvation: Cosmic and "For ALL"

Salvation in Christianity is always thought about in anthropocentric terms. It is common to think that God's salvation is only for humans and the rest of creation is not part of it. Salvation in cosmic terms was the subject matter of various meetings of the World Council of Churches' (WCC) Commission on World Mission and Evangelism (CWME) over the years. It emerged from relating salvation to social concerns (1952) and social salvation (1973) to envision cosmic salvation in 2013. The CWME document "Together Towards Life: Mission and Evangelism in Changing Landscapes," explains this cosmic salvation thus:[48]

> God did not send the Son for the salvation of humanity alone or give us a partial salvation. Rather the gospel is the good news for every part of creation and every aspect of our life and society. It is therefore vital to recognize God's mission in a cosmic sense and to affirm all life, the whole oikoumene, as being interconnected in God's web of life.

Inspired by the above document, Meehyun Chung further develops the theological idea that God always envisions cosmic salvation. Chung explains how the object of salvation is for all creation:

> God expects the holistic restoration of the oikos, which includes all creatures. Salvation means healing to restore the entire wounded world. Hence the event of the cross and resurrection brings about a healing process of the binary opposition between word and flesh, holy and secular, heaven and Earth, God's being and human being, word and flesh. Salvation understood as healing is the restoration of relationship at the level of the body, the individual, society, and the cosmos.[49]

Chung emphatically says that God's salvific process started from creation and that salvation through Jesus Christ embraces all of creation, including human beings and nature. "The love of the triune God is directed not only to human beings but also to the whole of the created world. Jesus Christ did not become flesh to bring partial salvation but came to Earth to offer full salvation. In other words, salvation through Jesus embraces all of creation, including human beings and nature. It reaches not only to the sentient being but also the insentient being."[50]

Hence, salvation should be understood in terms of eco-centred salvation; in more appropriate terms, it actually moves from human-centred salvation to life-centred salvation. The renewal of humans cannot be without the renewal of the whole creation. Life-centred salvation helps us to move from anthropocentric views of salvation to include the whole created world. Chung explains it thus: "God creates and sustains our universe, and human beings are not the rulers of this universe but a part of this universe. And as God is not only the creator of the universe—hence, the author and architect of *all* salvation—but also a God who goes out to his creation himself in self-donation, our ethical response, grounded in this recast vision of divinely oriented liberative and life-giving salvation, then is unlimited in scope and boundary."[51]

Finally, for Chung, the cosmic Christ encompasses humanity and earth together completely. The cosmic Christ restores the "original blessing" of the interrelated web of life and expands salvation to all creation. She says that the cosmic Christ gives cosmic soteriology, which is also "green salvation"—very much related to the social and ecological dimension of life.[52]

Hence envisioning salvation as cosmic and "for all" debunks the dominant Christian thinking that salvation is only for human beings.

Eschatology: The Hope for a Renewed World

Eschatology in Christian faith has always referred to death, judgement, end of the world, the final destiny of the human soul and the second coming of Jesus. For many, the destruction of the earth is a sign of the fulfilment of biblical prophecy. Such thinking does not encourage many Christians to commit themselves to save the earth. So there is a need to redefine eschatology.

With respect to climate justice, Solomon Victus identifies two major Christian positions on eschatology: otherworldly eschatology (which negates the earth) and this-worldly eschatology (which affirms the earth and wants to protect it).[53] For Victus, eschatology is important to address climate justice. "Climate justice is not simply an ecological justice; it is more of a socio-political and cultural justice. If we are ready to believe firmly in earthly eschatology, our theology needs to address all those aspects to attain climate justice." [54]

Victus offers by way of explanation how the new earth under the messianic rule (Isaiah 65: 17-25; Micah 4: 1-5) affirms a model of peaceful coexistence and creative usage of the discoveries of science. Victus says this realisable eschatology demands a new set of life principles: Minimum energy (entropy), minimum comforts, decentralised structures, democratic participation, collective decision-making, degrowth economy, and limits to consumption.[55] According to him, we need to keep alive the hope of a realisable eschatology and our efforts should be to find alternatives to redeem the earth for the establishment of a new heaven and new earth.

Rearticulating our faith is an urgent task in the context of neoliberal economic situations and globalisation. Victus emphasises that "heaven is also in a peaceless situation as long as the earth is boiling."[56] Deriving from Denis Edwards, he calls for an "ecological conversion" involving people from all kinds of ethnic, political and religious backgrounds. He urges the church to humbly take its stance alongside people and groups who have long led the way in ecological convictions and practice.[57]

In times of climate change and earth-shattering experiences, it is important to have a Christian eschatological vision which gives hope of an alternative world.

Barbara Rossing speaks about an "eschatological imagination" that creates a "counter-world."[58] Rossing uses a report by Joby Warrick and Chris Mooney on the "Effects of Climate Change" to point out how we live in an eschatological moment. According to this report, "the world crossed an eschatological threshold in 2016: we became the final generation of humans to ever breathe air with concentrations of carbon dioxide under 400 parts per million. Carbon dioxide levels have increased by more than 40 per cent since the advent of the Industrial Revolution, caused by the burning of fossil fuels. Now that the word 'irreversible' begins to be used in scientific reports about climate change, science itself becomes eschatological."[59]

More and more people are living in despair and hopelessness and hence "like the little daughter who is ill, who is at the eschatos, in Mark 5, we need healing."[60] Adopting a new approach to explain climate change in terms of sickness and healing, she says: "The world is ill; we are making ourselves sick. We need healing."[61]

Christian doctrines on God, human, sin, salvation and eschatology from a climate change perspective give greater theological foundation for the church to bear witness in today's context. We need the commitment, imagination, creativity and courage to expose the anthropocentric bias of our received doctrines and reclaim and reformulate the basic tenets of our faith from the vantage point of the earth and the earth community. That will enable the church to realise the manifestations of the creative and redemptive work of the Creator God in our midst, discern the implications of our vocation to "till and to keep" the earth, repent our ecological sins, and to broaden our understanding of salvation which embraces the whole inhabited earth.

Endnotes

[1] Karen L. Bloomquist (ed.), *God, Creation and Climate Change. Spiritual and Ethical Perspectives,* (Geneva: LWF Studies, 2009), 15-16.

[2] Sallie McFague, *A New Climate for Theology: God, The World, and Global Warming* (Minneapolis: Fortress Press, 2008), 72.

[3] Ibid., 73.

[4] Ibid., 75.

[5] Ibid., 76.

[6] Ibid., 77.

[7] Ibid., 79.

[8] Timothy Gorringe, "The Trinity," in *Systematic Theology and Climate Change: Ecumenical Perspectives*, edited by Michael S. Northcott and Peter M. Scott (New York: Routledge, 2014), 19.

[9] Karen L. Bloomquist, "What do You See, Feel, Believe in the face of Climate Change," in *God, Creation and Climate Change. Spiritual and Ethical Perspectives*, edited by Karen L. Bloomquist, (Geneva: LWF Studies, 2009), 19.

[10] It is a Greek word meaning mutual interpenetration. It was first used by the Cappadocian fathers to explain the doctrine of Trinity.

[11] Paulos Gregorios, *The Human Presence: An Orthodox View of Nature*, (Geneva: World Council of Churches, 1978), 78.

[12] Ibid., 88.

[13] Sallie McFague, *A New Climate for Theology*, (Minneapolis: Fortress Press, 2008), 59

[14] Ibid., 49.

[15] Ibid., 53.

[16] Ibid., 58.

[17] Larry L. Rasmussen, *Earth Community Earth Ethics*, (Maryknoll, New York: Orbis Books, 1996), 232.

[18] Ibid., 232.

[19] Ibid., 236.

[20] Ibid., 239

[21] Ibid., 239.

[22] Ibid., 242 – 244.

[23] Ibid., 280.

[24] Cynthia Moe-Lobeda, *Resisting Structural Evil: Love as Ecological-Economic Vocation*, (Minneapolis: Fortress Press, 2013),199.

[25] Ibid., 199.

[26] Ibid., 199.

[27] Ibid., 199.

[28] Neils Henrik Gregersen, "Christology," in *Systematic Theology and Climate Change: Ecumenical Perspectives*, edited by Michael S. Northcott and Peter M. Scott, (New York: Routledge, 2014), 36.

[29] Ibid., 36.

[30] Ibid., 40.

[31] Ibid., 42.

[32] Ibid., 45.

[33] Cynthia Moe-Lobeda, "Cross, Resurrection and the Indwelling God," in *God, Creation and Climate Change. Spiritual and Ethical Perspectives*, edited by Karen L. Bloomquist, (Geneva: LWF Studies, 2009), Ibid., 152.

[34] Ibid., 156.

[35] Moe-Lobeda takes this theology from Luther's theological works such as *The Travail of the Nature*, and *The Sacrament of the Body and the Blood of Christ*, 156-157.

[36] Samuel Rayan, "The Earth is the Lord's," in *Ecotheology: Voices from South and North,* David G. Hallman, ed., (New York: WCC/Orbis books, 1994), 130-146.

[37] Ibid., 131-146.

[38] Kirsteen Kim, "Bread and Breath in India: A Mission Pneumatology of Samuel Rayan", http://www.cccw.cam.ac.uk/media/documents/Archive/SeminarPapers/1999-2002/Bread and Breath in India The Mission Pneumatology of Samuel.pdf, accessed on 24 Jan 2020.

[39] Kirsteen Kim, Op.cit, 10.

[40] Cynthia Moe-Lobeda, "The Spirit as Moral-Spiritual Power for Earth-Honoring, Justice-Seeking Ways of Shaping Our Life in Common," in *Planetary Solidarity: Global Women's Voice on Christian Doctrine and Climate Justice* edited by Grace Ji-Sun Kim and Hilda P. Koster, (Minneapolis: Fortress Press, 2017), 250.

[41] Ibid., "The Spirit as Moral-Spiritual Power for Earth-Honoring," 254.

[42] Ibid., 254-256.

[43] Ibid., 269.

[44] Ibid., 272.

[45] Ibid., 59.

[46] Ibid., 60.

[47] Ibid., 62.

[48] Together towards Life: Mission and Evangelism in Changing Landscapes, file:///Users/vinodwesley/Downloads/Together_towards_Life.pdf, accessed on 10 Feb 2020.

[49] Meehyun Chung, "Salvation for All! Cosmic Salvation for an Age of Climate Injustice: A Korean Perspective," in *Planetary Solidarity: Global Women's Voice on Christian Doctrine and Climate Justice* edited by Grace Ji-Sun Kim and Hilda P. Koster, (Minneapolis: Fortress Press, 2017), 228.

[50] Ibid., 228.

[51] Ibid., 232-233.

[52] Ibid., 233.

[53] Solomon Victus, "New Heaven and New Earth: Towards Climate Justice," in *Religion and Society*, Vol. 56 No. 3-4, Sept-Dec. 2011, 74.

[54] Ibid., 74.

[55] Solomon Victus, "Key Hurdles of Eco-Theology in Theological Discourse," in *Margins in Conversation: Methodological Discourses in Theological Disciplines,* Op.cit., 75.

[56] Solomon Victus, "New Heaven and New Earth: Towards Climate Justice," Op.cit., 77.

[57] Solomon Victus, "Key Hurdles of Eco-Theology in Theological Discourse," in *Margins in Conversation: Methodological Discourses in Theological Disciplines,* Op.cit, 184.

[58] Barbara R. Rossing, "Reimagining Eschatology: Toward Healing and Hope for a World at the Eschatos," in *Planetary Solidarity: Global Women's Voices on Christian Doctrine and Climate Justice*, edited by Grace Ji-Sun Kim and Hilda P. Koster (Minneapolis: Fortress Press, 2017), 329.

[59] Ibid., 327.

[60] Ibid., 341.

[61] Ibid., 341.

Chapter 4

Women and Climate Change

Women and children are the worst victims of climate change. According to an Oxfam report, women make up for 70 per cent of those living below the poverty line who are the most affected by climate change. But when it comes to adapting to climate change, they are left out of the conversation and are unable to participate in the decision-making. This section will address how climate change affects women, their agency to address climate change, ecofeminist theological articulations, and eco-womanist and other theological contributions by women.

In many South Asian communities, women play several roles as workers in agriculture or other informal sectors. Fetching water and fuel is considered a woman's job so much so that we see, in many arid and underdeveloped areas, long lines of women walking with pails of water and bundles of fuel wood. They also have a major role as caretakers, to look after the children, the sick and the elderly, in addition to managing the home and its assets.

So, when disaster hits, women find it difficult to leave the house and migrate to look for shelter and work. Floods, droughts and storms also put great stress on them physically and psychologically. Then, there is always the danger of girls dropping out of school to save on school fees or to do household chores.

It is patriarchy and socially constructed roles and responsibilities that usually put women at a disadvantage. Climate change exacerbates existing social inequalities, leaving women disproportionately vulnerable to it. For instance, women are very dependent for their livelihood on natural resources that are threatened by climate change. Statistics say that during natural disasters, women and children are 14 times more likely to die than men. When it comes to women farmers, they have limited access to natural resources and limited access to information and services about climate-resilient and adaptive agricultural strategies and technologies. Social, economic and political barriers too limit the participation of women in decision-making and their coping capacity with respect to climate change.[1]

According to the Women's Earth and Climate Action Network (WECAN), women accounted for 61 per cent of the fatalities caused by Cyclone Nargis in Myanmar in 2008, 70-80 per cent in the 2004 Indian Ocean tsunami, and 91 per cent in the 1991 cyclone in Bangladesh.[2] A study conducted by the Urban Institute in South Asia's slums in Delhi, Dhaka, Islamabad and Lahore shows that women were highly affected from frequent torrential rain and diseases like dengue and chikungunya that come with it. Floods and heatwaves also made it impossible for them to find work for a long time.[3]

At the same time, with the efforts of many organisations to create sensitivity towards gender justice, women have proved that they can be powerful agents in addressing climate change. Women have helped devise effective climate change solutions that build stronger communities. For example, in a CARE project in Bangladesh, women prioritised climate preparedness strategies such as homestead gardening and duck rearing that could be implemented close to homes; in the project, which recruited female field officers, women made up 58 per cent of the total project participants.[4] Oxfam America points out several such examples of women's initiatives at national and community levels in situations of climate crisis all over the world.

Ecofeminist Theological Perspective

Women's theological response to climate change began with the beginning of ecofeminism[5] and ecofeminist theology in the 1970s. It emerged out of a recognition that the tendency to exploit the environment is the same attitude of patriarchal societies to dominate and exploit women. While ecofeminism emphasises the connection between the exploitation of the earth and women, it also seeks to prove that women can theologically and praxiologically envision and reimagine a world with equality and justice. Several women have contributed to this ecofeminist theological articulation. This section introduces a few of them.

Eco-theology and Women's Struggles

Women's movements all over the world have been struggling to protect the rights of women and the earth. Gabriele Dietrich, through her writings and engagements with various people's movements in India, especially women's movements, has contributed greatly to Indian ecofeminist theology. She says that women engaged in survival struggles are simultaneously struggling for the protection of nature. According to her, women and nature are intimately related and so their domination and liberation are similarly linked.[6] She discovers an affinity between the subjugation of nature and the subordination of women.[7]

With the help of the life stories of the women of the fishing community and slum-dwellers, she proves how patriarchy and caste are entrenched in women's work and control over their bodies (treating her as a commodity), curtailing her relationship with nature and constraining her spiritual expressions, which "subjugates her physically, emotionally and silences and distances her epistemologically."[8]

Like many other theologians, Dietrich also considers Sallie Mcfague's metaphor of the "world as the body of God" as an important theological framework to address life struggles. She says, "It [world as the body of God] indicates a perspective in which the interactions between spirit and world is vital. God's spirit is not accessible to us outside the body which is the world. The world again is not just nature, good creation, but also society, the way human beings are interacting with each other and with nature. Exploitation and violence are thus a disease of the body of God, inflicted by a violation of the Spirit which safeguards life in Freedom and Sustenance."[9] According to Dietrich, nature can be redeemed only when society is liberated from its unjust structures. Exegeting various women's struggles and the promises bestowed through women in the biblical narratives, Dietrich affirms that "the earth is allied with the women and the Messianic promise. The labors of women, in Childbirth and by the work of her hands, will be redeemed by breaking down the patriarchal conditions of productions of life in the New Community of the people of God which will be rescued by an alliance with the earth."[10]

Deriving from the biblical catchphrase "Earth is the Lord's and the fullness thereof," which also implies "the world and those who dwell therein" (Ps 24:1), Dietrich says, "It is not a question of the world being God's property but the world and those who dwell therein being the material expression of the spirit. It is in this light that neither the earth nor human beings can be owned or possessed. Women, children and slaves cannot be anyone's property nor can the earth or the sea be."[11]

For Dietrich, the sabbath rest (Deut 5: 14–15), release of slaves and debts (Deut 15), the law on tithes (Deut 14: 22-29) and the jubilee year characterised by the redistribution of land (Lev 25) are important biblical imperatives for the protection of the poor and the earth. She argues that the jubilee vision is diametrically opposed to the policies that privatise and commercialise land, sea, rivers, and even drinking water.[12]

Dietrich considers McFague's metaphors of God as *Mother*, God as *Lover*, and God as *Friend* as having rich theological significance for ecological thinking. Motherhood is connected with the protection of life and subsistence production, the labour of women and workers in the unorganised sectors of society, but this mothering and nurturing is controlled by patriarchal science and technology and privatised socioeconomic policies, which is at the root of the ongoing ecological destruction. According to her, "If we recognize God as Mother, the motherhood and nurture must also be the guiding principle of reorganisation of economic and political structures."[13]

Similarly, for Dietrich, God as Lover identifies love with responsibility, loyalty and truthfulness, not in patriarchal forms but in forms of joyfulness, praise and thanksgiving which translates itself into a lasting concern for the sustenance of life.[14] God as Friend breaks the barriers of caste, family, political affiliation and cultural identity. Dietrich notes that the risen Christ met his disciples in Emmaus as a friend and asked them to share something to eat. This, Dietrich explains, "…is the promise of the presence as a friend which holds the ecological vision of an economy of sharing in which life on earth can be sustained in solidarity."[15]

Eco-centred Feminist Spirituality

Every local culture has significant religious and spiritual concepts and beliefs that are ecologically enriching. Christian theology many a time does not give credence to such valuable religious ideas in local traditions. Ecofeminit thinkers and theologians have always attempted to develop theories and theological thinking from such values. Aruna Gnanadason, a prominent ecofeminist theologian, draws on the Indian religious traditions of *Shakti, Annapurna* and *Aranyani* as symbols of power, nurture and sustenance in her writings on eco-centred feminist spirituality. She points out that ecofeminism is a holistic vision of interdependence between women and nature as between humanity and nature.[16]

She criticises the Western scientific worldview, informed by the Industrial Revolution and carefully implemented by the "development" paradigm, as the main reason for denigrating women's organic relationship with nature. Towards an ecofeminist theology, Gnanadason proposes a "feminist paradigm" emerging from various struggles of women in protecting the natural world and from eco-centred feminist spirituality. She quotes Vandana Shiva's interpretation of *Shakthi,* the feminine creative principle of cosmos, to explain how nature is important for theologising in India. She says, "This is a worldview personified by the re-emergence of the dynamic energy (*Shakti*), which is the source and substance of all things, pervading everything. Nature, both animate and inanimate, is thus an expression of *Shakti,* the feminine and creative principle of the cosmos. All forms of nature and life in nature are the forms, the children of the Mother of Nature who is nature itself born of creative play of her thought."[17] Gnanadason affirms that "nature is therefore symbolised as the embodiment of the feminist principle and must form the core of an Indian feminist eco-theology."[18]

For her, the *Annapurna* tradition, where the goddess nourishes the needy with vegetation produced from her own body, is also important for Indian ecofeminist theology.[19] Similarly, Gnanadason brings into attention the practice of worshipping *Aranyani*, the goddess of the forest, the primary source of life and fertility, as the organising principle of Indian civilisation. For Gnanadason, the holistic vision of our spiritual past is an important source for ecofeminist theology in India. She expounds:

> It is such a holistic vision based in our spiritual past, that eco-feminist theology draws inspiration from, in India. This 'other voice' which calls for change, growth and transformation must be heeded as we attempt to develop an authentic eco-theology in the Indian context. The feminist paradigm offers an alternative vision of hope and calls for a recovery of the feminine principle, as respect for life in nature and society seems to be the only way forward, the only hope for the world.... It is a challenge coming out of women's lived experiences by not only weeping, with nature, for deliverance and freedom but out of years of organized resistance against senseless destruction.[20]

According to Gnanadason, women have not just been merely passive victims of ecological destruction but have also been at the forefront of resistance and protests. Way back in the 1730s in Khejadli in Rajasthan in India, women protested against the cutting of sacred trees.[21] Similarly, the Chipko movement in the early 1970s in India was led by women and children who did not allow trees to be cut down for industrialisation. This perspective of women is important in recognising the holistic redemption of *oikos,* or God's household. Rather than ecofeminism being simply a romantic or esoteric endeavour, Gnanadason says it is important to acknowledge that it is women, the poor, the Dalits and Adivasis (indigenous people) who maintain the "traditions of prudent care" of the resources of the earth and also to draw lessons from the epistemologies of the subaltern peoples of our country-wisdom which we have tended to ignore.[22]

Gnanadason believes it is necessary and possible to reclaim Christianity as an earth faith by deconstructing certain aspects of the faith tradition. Ecofeminist theologians critique the dualism between mind and body, man and woman, and human beings and nature. They envision the liberation of the poor and nature as two sides of the same coin and prefer more organic images of God than "God The Father" or monarchical ideas of God which are very aggressive and human-centred.[23]

Gnanadason, deriving from Mcfague, challenges us to go beyond a subject-object relationship with God and the earth to a subject-subject relationship affirming the intrinsic value, integrity and goodness of all creation. Pointing out that the Bible has such images, she defines God in terms of relationality: "I see God as the compassionate earth-loving parent; a resisting, struggling poor woman; God as one who brooks no injustice and who protects the earth; God as a community, as the inextricable link between the divine and the earth and most importantly God as mothering, the nurturing woman, is perhaps the most crucial for our times."[24]

Life-centred Theological Paradigm

Ivy Singh, another Indian feminist theologian, says that ecofeminist theology must take into account the world of the suffering of women and nature as well as their resources and express solidarity with their struggles and celebrate their contributions. She adds that ecofeminism must be comprehensive in its perspective of liberation, which will ensure the overall liberation of women along with the ecosystem, and prepare them sufficiently for the establishment of a just society. She affirms that throughout the history of humankind, God, women and the earth have kept their faithful roles as providers, protectors and nurtures of life.

Ivy Singh proposes the idea of a "life-centred theological paradigm" as against the anthropocentric theological paradigm:

> Life-centered theological paradigm in which God's entire creation including women and nature will become the subject of theologizing. The "Life-centred theological paradigm" is inclusive, because it brings all God's creation as all "groaning for liberation." … This life-centered paradigm is dialogical because it will not draw upon a single women's experience or ecological problem, rather it takes into serious consideration and concentrates on the inter-dependence and inter-connectedness between women and nature. This paradigm will also use and draw new insights from various religious resources for sustaining and upholding 'life.'[25]

She further proposes the idea of ecofeminism as a sacramental theology. Women's work and nature's products are used for sacraments in churches.[26] The elements of the Eucharist, bread and wine, are the produce of the land and produced by hard work, especially of women. Thus the sharing of bread and wine signifies the sharing of land resources and is about the remembrance of the toil and sweat of people. For Ivy Singh, this faith signifying life and land as sacraments provide a new ecumenical vision for Christian theology, moving towards an ecumenism of "the household of God."[27] She asserts that this life-centred spirituality and theology, focusing on the redemption of all, is future-oriented in the sense that it demands responsibility in not plundering resources meant for future generations.

One of her significant ideas is that ecofeminism is missionary theology. According to her, "It [ecofeminism] acknowledges God's mission as holistic and cosmic in nature. Its aim is not geographic, territorial and numerical expansion, but the transformation of the whole cosmos. In such a cosmic mission, God's entire creation, including women and nature, interpenetrate each other, uphold each other, strengthen each other and sustain each other."[28] In which case, the theology of ecofeminism will emerge as an authentic, inclusive and praxis-oriented Indian Christian liberative living theology.

Dalit/Subaltern Women: Agents of Transformation

At one stage of the evolution of ecofeminism, it occurred that ecofeminism does not include the voices of Dalits and Adivasis who work closely with land and nature. At the same time some of the religious and spiritual ideas that were adopted in ecofeminism were that of the dominant castes and religions. This realisation led to the emergence of another concept called organic womanism, which is based on the knowledge and experiences of Dalit and Adivasi women. Geevarghese Coorilos Nallunakkal, a prominent Orthodox theologian, popularised the concept of organic womanism in India. He was able to develop this concept with his deep engagement with the grassroots movements in India. This concept particularises 'women'; it is the Dalit and Adivasi women interacting with land (ecology) that constitutes the core of organic womanism. Dalits and Adivasis are deeply concerned about the preservation of their own land, space and therefore about their own ecology. Innate in Dalit and Adivasi ethos is a strong attachment to the image of mother. But this idea of mother is very different from the idea of a benevolent mother who has to sacrifice her life for the benefit of her family; rather, this relationship is very interactive aimed at the survival and sustenance of both nature and her children.[29] This survival and sustenance is the social justice component (eco-justice) in the life of organic women.[30]

The struggle against climate change by Dalit women in different parts of India exhibit this aspect. Dalit women are akin to the Samaritan woman (at the well) who initiates new discourses emerging out of their oppressive structures to save the world. Dalit women exhibit the same passion, intuition, courage, and the sharing of the gospel as that of the Samaritan woman for the liberation of the community. They who live with the earth—'the organic women'—have the living waters, i.e, the solution to save the communities on earth from the victimisation of human greed with their sustainable and organic methods.

Here are some examples. Dalit women in India from Medak, Andhra Pradesh, have sown the seeds of hope in the neighbouring region of Vidarbha in Maharashtra, which has seen a spate of farmer suicides over the years. These women have enriched local people by teaching them alternative farming ideas and good agricultural practices.[31] Dalit women in Zaheerabad, Andhra Pradesh, through a collective of 5,000 women spread across 75 villages in arid, interior regions, have proposed a chemical-free, non-irrigated, organic agriculture as one method to combat global warming.[32] They intersperse crops and use farmyard manure which yields good results.

Case Study: Tamil Nadu Women's Collective

Tamil Nadu Women's Collective (TWC) was started in 1994 as a grassroots initiative in the state of Tamil Nadu in south India. It is now a collective of more than 150,000 Dalit women.

TWC practices and promotes agroecology, which is an organic and budget-free agricultural method of growing many crops, such as grains, lentils, beans and oilseeds, together to sustain biodiversity.[33] Its objective is to help poor women attain self-reliance and autonomy and to combat climate change by using adaptive and organic agricultural methods. This women's collective provides an alternative organic model for the Indian agricultural economy, which is increasingly getting dominated by the capitalist agri-industry.

Over the last 10 years, members of TWC have been engaged in joint and individual efforts (at local, state and national levels) to ensure local food and water security through sustainable methods. The women have built on their traditional knowledge to enhance productivity and sustainability. Their interventions to selectively and carefully introduce both traditional and modern practices are synergistic, thereby bringing together an "adaptation strategy" and a "mitigation strategy."

TWC's approach goes alongside the ecowomanist methodology elucidated by Melanie Harris in her outstanding work *EcoWomanism: African American Women and Earth-Honoring Faiths*. It is about how subaltern women all over the world are connected in their commitment and work to challenge climate change. Harris outlines seven steps to put into practice ecowomanist analysis: 1) Honouring experience and mining ecomemory; 2) critical reflection of experience and ecomemory; 3) womanist intersectional analysis; 4) critically examining history and tradition; 5) engaging transformation; 6) sharing dialogue; and 7) taking action for earth justice.

This ecowomanist method follows a spiral pattern (as against a linear one) where steps are interchangeable. It is both a deconstructivist and a constructivist approach. The analysis from one step dovetails and expands into another.[34] According to Harris, this method is intersectional, interdisciplinary and its approach is political, liberationist, theological, and religio-spiritual with a social justice agenda for earth justice.[35] Furthermore, it combines resources and methods from various fields such as environmental studies, ethics, sociology, religion, anthropology, agricultural studies, history, geology, health, medicine and more. The analytical framework is basically of race-class-gender.[36] Harris' methodology involved the analysis of ecowisdom in the African and African-American contexts. Let us analyse the work of TWC using the methodology of Harris.

Honouring Experience and Mining Ecomemory: Shiney Varghese, in her study on TWC, mentions how the memories of women like Kaliammal (Sangupuaram village), Ponnuthai (Santhapatti village) and Sahayamary (Thotikalai village) regarding crop selection in their villages and families were utilised to rekindle their agency to fight ecological challenges posed by climate change.[37] They were able to retrieve memories of the crop varieties that were used for sustainable agriculture many years ago. These memories were hidden or the knowledges forgotten in the pursuit of producing hybrid crops for the market economy.

Critical Reflection of Dalit Experience and Ecomemory: Dalits' experience with the earth are defined my hardship and oppression. Many Dalit women in TWC remember their stories of abuse in their lives. But their stories also show how their relationship with the earth served as a healing experience for them. A news portal describes the story of Kasiammal of Erachi in Tamil Nadu as follows:

> Farming wasn't the only area of Kasiammal's life in which she did what she was told. The former kuli [daily wage laborer] grew up at a time when "untouchable" was still an acceptable term.

She remembers removing her shoes when walking through an upper-caste neighborhood, and never asking for a dog, which was forbidden for Dalits, lest their pets mate with those belonging to higher-caste owners. In the fields, when landowners and their sons came to fetch kuli girls "to do what they wanted with them," Kasiammal says, she knew to keep her mouth shut.

Despite the narrow canal of sewage that runs from the upper-caste neighborhood to her home in Erachi's Dalit section and her uneven access to potable water, Kasiammal says things have changed. "We have this," she says, pointing her chin toward the soil.[38]

Womanist Intersectional Analysis: The third step involves reflecting on the experiences and making an analysis of the interconnected nature of social categorisations such as race, class and gender. In an interview, Sheelu Francis, one of the founders and president of TWC, points out how casteism combined with colonialism devastated the traditional knowledge of Dalit communities on agriculture. She says, "The main values (sustainable agricultural knowledge) are already there; they are part of Indian culture. But the long exposure to Western colonial and imperial powers operated many changes and in many cases, people became alienated from their cultural roots."[39] TWC members were among the first women to attend the monthly farmers' meetings held by the state of Tamil Nadu. The officials, thinking they had come to the wrong place for widow pension or some such, guided them to the social welfare department. But soon they realised that they were TWC women who had come for the farmers' meeting.[40]

One of the main works of TWC is to bring marginalised women to the decision-making table. Women's voices are silenced in many different areas of life, especially in terms of economic policies, developmental projects and politics. In the context of climate crisis, women's participation in decision-making assumes significance.

Examining History and Tradition: Sheelu Francis points out how the Green Revolution[41] and the agricultural policies in India destroyed traditional farming and prompted a shift from producing millet to producing rice.[42] Caste, too, has a role to play in this shift. Many women in Tamil Nadu who have traditionally grown millets are Dalits, whereas rice is associated with lighter-skinned people and the upper castes. Sheelu Francis identifies the intersection of government policies and caste hegemony in causing this shift as follows:

> In the process of trying to reach the upper caste, you change your diet, and then you change your agriculture. And the government policies pushed hybrid seeds and chemical fertilizers and pesticides for rice production, as well as a minimum support price for rice. This has pushed millet out of production. And everyone is maximizing water from the ground for rice. Even the government only distributes rice and wheat for people in need of food.[43]

Caste and gender oppression which affected Dalit women's lives also gave them restricted access to natural resources like land, water and seeds. "Land is a very big issue for TWC. Even among our TWC members, only 10 per cent have their land. Ninety per cent are landless labourers," says Sheelu Francis.[44]

TWC wants the government to give single women long-term leases to unutilised land owned by companies. TWC organises women farmers, particularly widows who are landless, into collective farming where they lease land and grow millet, which first ensures food security at the household level.[45] Says Sheelu Francis: "The three things that we say, the first is land, the second is traditional seeds, which is very important, and the third is animals. And, of course, water. These are the things we are trying to focus on."[46]

Engaging Transformation: Transformation in terms of climate change can take place when the scientific world is ready to learn and adopt from the knowledge (ecoknowledge) of communities that live very close to nature. Kancha Ilaiah, a prominent Dalit scholar and historian, says that Dalit ecoknowledge sprouts from their spiritual and scientific realm. Contrasting it with the Brahminical (upper caste) Hindu belief which considers manual productive labour lower than spiritual practices, Kancha Ilaiah explains Dalit ecospirituality as follows:

> The Dalit life process provides a positive direction to evolve and adopt a positive religious course as well, as it does not see any contradiction in the production of manure and its link with God's spiritual realm. Further, a spiritual ideology has to interact with the scientific process, as spirituality and science are closely related. The Mala (a Dalit Caste) mode of thought possesses that understanding of the relationship between science and spirituality—that is why the Malas spent their days working in the fields and making manure and went to the temples that they built near the village in the evenings. The Hindu temples, on the other hand, do not allow any productive community to set foot inside them.[47]

He goes on to say that even the irrigation process of the Dalit communities in agriculture was based on a teleological ethic, where the future of the community is very important for them.[48]

Sharing Knowledge through Dialogue: This step affirms the belief that that the earth is a concern for all religions and that most religious traditions embody an earth ethic that can guide an individual's faith and earth orientation.[49] To date, TWC has had no interreligious sharing of knowledge. Nevertheless, TWC is very much aware of and participates in dialogue on global and national efforts for agroecological approaches and multifunctional agriculture.[50]

Taking Action for Earth Justice: Teaching Ecowomanism: The seventh step involves teaching ecowomanism. TWC also gives emphasis on pedagogy and preparing teaching material for teaching students in schools and colleges. Multilevel education in health and farming is an important aspect of TWC. Sheelu Francis explains this component as follows:

> We are trying to educate people on different levels. Even if they are not producers, we are trying to educate them about the nutritious content of millet. Women are seeing the health of their families suffer, so when we offer millet as a nutritious alternative, they adopt it quickly. We have a high school and college program about millet, which includes a cooking contest that emphasizes nutrition.[51]

Also, in order to resist the agrarian crisis in India rooted in the Green Revolution and caste system, TWC proposes and practices agroecology. Sheelu Francis explains this as follows:

> The Collective uses agroecology—which they also call 'natural farming' or 'zero budget' farming—to address the issues faced by women and their families. When we were working with the women, we came across lots of cases of cancer, and we linked these health problems to their food intake, especially to food produced using chemical fertilizers and pesticides. This is why we thought to go back to natural and traditional way of farming.[52]

Thus we can see today that Dalit women and many poor women who live close to nature, especially those in the agricultural field, are actively engaged in the work of transformation. These women are a great source of encouragement for all of us and they exude hope that we can challenge and work against climate change and protect vulnerable communities. TWC represents many other grassroots movements in South Asia and all over the world in dedicating their life to renew this earth and provide a sustainable life for all. It is imperative on the eco-theology movement in India to listen to their voices and become intersectional in their approach, engaging with the overlapping and interdependent systems of discrimination, oppression and disadvantage.

Endnotes

[1] https://www.mrfcj.org/wp-content/uploads/2015/11/MRFCJ-_Womens-Participation-An-Enabler-of-Climate-Justice_2015.pdf

[2] https://www.wecaninternational.org/why-women, accessed on 5 Feb 2020.

[3] https://www.urban.org/urban-wire/south-asian-slums-women-face-consequences-climate-change, accessed on 5 Feb 2020.

[4] https://www.oxfamamerica.org/static/media/files/climatechangewomen-factsheet.pdf, accessed on 10 Jan 2020.

[5] The term ecofeminism was first used by the French writer Francoise D'Eaubonne in 1974. She used it to signify a woman's potential to bring about an environmental change to ensure human survival. Ecofeminism is an attempt to synthesise two separated struggles, feminism and ecology. Ecofeminism is a movement that sees the exploitation of nature as intimately linked to the exploitation of women. Ecofeminists resist patriarchy and the process of globalisation which affects both women and nature (see Ivy, 208). Ecofeminism identifies women with nature as victims of the dominating structure: for women, it is experienced as sexism, discrimination, inequality, and so on; for nature, this is experienced as exploitation, pollution, destruction of forests, and the like. They note that practically women are the first victims of ecological crisis since their work depends directly on the availability of natural resources (see Aruna Gnanadason, "Women, Economy and Ecology," in David G. Hallman, ed., *Ecotheology*, 180.

[6] Gabriele Dietrich, "Women's Perspective on Ecology," in *Religion and Society*, Vol. XXXVII, No.2, June 1990, 55-56.

[7] Gabriele Dietrich, "Ethnicity, Ecology & Feminism," in *AJTR*, VI, 1, Jan-June, 1993, 38.

[8] Gabriele Dietrich, *A New Thing on Earth*, (Delhi: ISPCK, 2001), 176-186.

[9] Ibid., 187.

[10] Ibid., 190.

[11] Ibid., 193.

[12] Ibid., 194-195.

[13] Ibid., 200.

[14] Ibid., 201.

[15] Gabriele Dietrich., 201.

[16] Ibid., "Women, Economy and Ecology," in *Ecotheology*, edited by David G. Hallman, op. cit., 183.

[17] Aruna Gnanadason, "Towards a Feminist Eco-theology for India," in *Ecology and Development: Theological Perspectives*, Op.cit, 30-31.

[18] She is also careful in pointing out the criticism that such linking of women with nature may reinforce the subordination of women and reduce women only to the mothering-nurturing roles.Ibid., 31

[19] *Annapurna* is a vegetation goddess. Her body (*Annapurna*) is the earth, source of plant-life and all that lives. *Annapurna* is the vital force concerned with the growth of crops, the plenitude of food and the nourishing sap of all being.Ibid.,36.

[20] Aruna Gnanadason, "Towards a Feminist Eco-theology for India," in *Ecology and Development: Theological Perspectives*, Op.cit, 37.

[21] Women, men and children led by Amritha Devi had stopped the Maharaja of Jodhpur's men from cutting the sacred trees of their village.

[22] Aruna Gnanadason, "The Struggle to Survive: Women and Environmental Justice–A Theological Response," in *Religion and Society: Ecology and Environment*, Vol. 56 No. 3-4, Sept-Dec. 2011. 48.

[23] Ibid., 48-54.

[24] Ibid., 54.

[25] Ivy Singh," *Eco-feminism as a Paradigm Shift in Theology*," in IJT 45/1&2, 2003, http://www.biblicalstudies.org.uk/pdf/ijt/45_015.pdf, accessed on 5 Jan 2020.

[26] Ibid., 26–27.

[27] Ibid., 27.

[28] Ibid., 27.

[29] Organic womanism in a way criticises the Western, middle class and, at times, elitist brand of ecofeminism, a perspective that would address the issue of women and nature, particularly from a Dalit/tribal perspective, not merely from the perspective of women in an unqualified sense. The adjective 'organic' is engaged here to highlight the natural relationship that Dalit and tribal women have with nature, which women of the middle class

and other sections of society do not possess at the same level and intensity. Geevarghese Coorilos Nalunnakkal, *Ethical Issues: Subaltern Perspectives* (Tiruvalla: CSS, 2007), 92 – 111.

[30] The mother and her children own each other. Both women and nature assume the role of each other, owning and caring for each other. Motherhood here represents creativity, regeneration and sustenance. Organic womanism stands out also on account of its revolutionary political praxis. Organic womanism and organic environmentalism is a form of subaltern identity politics. This is a point of departure for organic womanism because it is about victims taking leadership of their struggles and articulating their worldviews. Ibid., 107.

[31] http://southasia.oneworld.net/fromthegrassroots/Dalit-farm-women-offer-tips-to-vidharba, accessed on 10 Jan 2020

[32] Women Farmers Ready to Beat Climate Change, http://ipsnews.net/news.asp?idnews=46131, accessed on 10 Jan 2020.

[33] https://www.alternet.org/food/womens-collective-using-agroecology-fight-indias-green-revolution, accessd on 10 Jan 2020.

[34] Melanie L. Harris. *Ecowomanism: African American Women and Earth-Honoring Faiths* (Maryknoll:Orbis Books, 2017)., 10-16.

[35] Ibid., 19.

[36] Ibid., 19-20.

[37] Shiney Varghese, "Women at the Centre of Climate-friendly Approaches to Agriculture and Water Use," https://www.iatp.org/files/451_2_107914.pdf, accessed on 2 Feb 2020.

[38] http://america.aljazeera.com/features/2014/6/from-untouchabletoorganicDalitwomensowchangeinindia.html, accessed on 2 Feb 2020.

[39] Interview of Sheelu Francis, Tamil Nadu Women's Collective, Tamil Nadu–India, http://www.socioeco.org/bdf_fiche-document-1594_en.html, accessed on 2 Feb 2020.

[40] http://america.aljazeera.com/features/2014/6/from-untouchabletoorganicDalitwomensowchangeinindia.html, accessed on 2 Feb 2020.

[41] The Green Revolution was introduced in post-independent India to address its food crisis in the 1960s. It is intensive chemical-based agriculture following the Western agricultural model. Though it solved the food crisis issue at that time it resulted in polluting the land and affecting the environment. http://edugreen.teri.res.in/explore/bio/green.htm, accessed on 2 Feb 2020.

[42] https://www.alternet.org/food/womens-collective-using-agroecology-fight-indias-green-revolution, accessed on 2 Feb 2020.

[43] https://www.alternet.org/food/womens-collective-using-agroecology-fight-indias-green-revolution, accessed on 2 Feb 2020.

[44] Ibid.,

[45] Ibid.,

[46] Ibid.,

[47] Kancha Ilaiah, *Post-Hindu India*, (New Delhi: Sage Publication, 2006), 61.

[48] Ibid., 62.

[49] Melanie L. Harris, 57.

[50] Shiney Varghese, "Women at the centre of Climate- friendly Approaches to agriculture and Water Use," https://www.iatp.org/files/451_2_107914.pdf (accessed on 2 April 2018).

[51] https://www.alternet.org/food/womens-collective-using-agroecology-fight-indias-green-revolution, accessed on 1 Feb 2020.

[52] Ibid.,

Chapter 5

Climate Justice and Christian Ethics

Christian ethics is ethical discernment and action on issues of moral ambiguity informed by contextually relevant epistemological sources. Today climate justice is an ethical issue. Christian ethics will enable us to critically analyse and confront the socio-economic structures that give rise to climate change. This section will highlight the contributions of Indian Christian theologians and ethicists such as K.C. Abraham and Felix Wilfred who bring in a Third World perspective to climate change ethics. It further draws from ethical reflections on ecological justice, neighbour love and subaltern grassroots movements to address climate change from a justice perspective.

A Third World Perspective

K.C. Abraham is an Indian Christian ethicist, whose perspectives on ecology, economics and ecumenism are significant in the context of climate change from a South Asian perspective. K.C. Abraham defines Chrsitian ethics as follows:

> Ethics, as distinct from morality or moral behaviour, is reflection on the basis of moral action. Why I ought to do? What I ought to do? The "why" becomes the reflective part and it provides

> the distinctive character to the discipline of ethics. Morality
> is a descriptive term, but ethics is a reflective, scientific study.
>
> Christian ethics is, therefore, a reflection on the Christian basis
> for moral action. Faith and works are inseparable. They are
> the presuppositions that mould our ethical judgement. A just
> God demands justice and righteousness; a dreaded God evokes
> responses of fear and awe. Faith in compassionate God sensitises
> us for caring action.[1]

In the context of the ecological crisis, he says that it is very
important to ask the following ethical questions:[2]

What type of community do/should we live in?

What type of communities are we building?

What kind of future has our earth?

Abraham stress the point that in every ecological discussion and
negotiation the perspective of justice should not be forgotten.
He says: "One American's consumption is equal to that of 8,150
Indians. One may have to make a distinction between survival
emission of the poor and the luxury emission of the rich."[3]
Hence, from a Third World perspective, "justice" becomes an
important concept in climate change discussions.

Concerned about the ethical right of non-human nature,
Abraham prophetically calls out to the church and people's
movements for possible responses. According to him, *oikos* is
the root of three important words that describe different areas of
our relationship. They are economics, ecology and ecumenics.[4]
These three terms are interrelated. *Oikos,* or the *ecumene,* is
not only the world of humans but of all living and non-living
things—the earth. It is here that the church, God's *ecumene,* is
called to fulfill its mission.[5]

According to Abraham, the problems of the poor and the concerns of the environment are inextricably intertwined. He views the ecological crisis as a justice issue. For him, ecojustice is also related to Christian mission. "The ecological perspective also challenges our notion of ethics. The ecological model of mutual interdependence can provide a new orientation in ethics that can be the source of human renewal. The new perspective affirms our interrelatedness to one another and nature."[6]

Abraham points out that a Third World perspective on ecology should seek to: One, address conflict of values, i.e. whom are we listening to? Is it to the proponents of "development" or its victims; two, envision the perspective of the poor which challenges the present civilisation of development; and three, heed to the prophetic demands of the poor or poor nations for justice, equity and fairness in the use of natural resources and also to engage in the negotiations for the future.[7]

Borrowing from Leonardo Boff's panentheistic idea of God, Abraham points out that, "The God experience is pervasive to our earth experience. God is present in all earthly experience enhancing our relationship."[8] Boff outlines the idea of cosmic dance, the dance of Shiva, as presenting the mystery of creation, which is a dance among creation, preservation, destruction, rest and redemption. This is not to reject the commitment to God of Christian revelation; rather, it asserts that, while the prophetic tradition of the biblical faith helps us to hear and respond to the cry of the poor, the Eastern mystical and cosmic tradition helps us to discern the cry of the earth and commit ourselves to its life.[9]

For Abraham, the rights of the non-human world are very important in the ecological discourse, and the essential aspect of human existence is to bond with the earth. In order to articulate the Christian understanding of the rights of the non-human world, Abraham alludes to the concept called "Theos-Rights."[10] That is to mean, creation exists for God; all living and non-living things exist for God and not for human beings. A profound ethical understanding of the non-human world will deepen our commitment to it and also help us realise that a disregard for the earth's resources is a violation of the inherent and God-given rights to them.

Abraham considers the six principles of hermeneutics proposed by Norman Habel from the book *Readings from the Perspective of the Earth* as significant in reading the Bible from an ethical and eco-justice perspective. These principles are as follows: the principle of intrinsic worth, the principle of interconnectedness, the principle of voice, the principle of purpose, the principle of mutual custodianship, and the principle of resistance. For Abraham, these principles provide a perspective in rereading the Bible from the perspective of the earth.[11]

For him, ecology from a justice perspective calls for a paradigm shift in our approach to ecumenism. He says, "Ecology of Ecumenism calls for a unity that is rooted in our current belonging to the earth. Creation is God's first act, not history. Reflection on God's first act helps us to recover our real origin and destiny as human creatures."[12] Ecumenism and ecology are about relationship and interrelatedness. Ecologically-oriented ecumenism favours an other-directed value system. In which case, Christian mission becomes the process of transformation from the demonic powers that destroy nature to the power of love that cares for it. To pollute God's creation is to go against God's purpose for us and God's world, says Abraham, and only in solidarity with the powerless and marginalised in their struggle for liberation and wholeness can we know and experience the God of love and mercy.[13]

Prophetic Eco-theology and Ecological Economics

Felix Wilfred, a Catholic theologian from India, speaks about prophetic eco-theology. According to him, eco-theology is prophetic inasmuch as it encourages people to raise their voices against climate injustice. He says:

> There is an intimate connection between the violence and gross disorder in our societies and the destruction of the environment. Ecotheology is to be viewed as a vision that is oriented towards the praxis of liberating nature and the poor from greed. Ecotheology helps us to re-enact creation by controlling the chaos of money and wealth are making in the life of society and of nature today. Ecotheology is inherently prophetic. It is the praxis of struggle, sustained by faith in God's creation, against the technocrats, state agencies, business interests, and the pundits of development."[14]

He points out that the prophetic nature of eco-theology cuts across religious traditions. Theology becomes a common endeavour as people of various religious traditions struggle together to challenge the destruction of the environment and damage to the human community. Interreligious eco-theology will try to imbue our approach to nature with a sense of sacredness (which is not to be confused with "sacralisation of nature") and a sense of wonder.[15]

Felix Wilfred points out that an earth community lives in communion, peace and harmony. It requires for us to go beyond the mere stewardship approach to nature, which would be still infected by anthropocentrism, and move towards *kinship with the earth*.[16] He critiques the dominant model of the market economy which is the cause for both social inequality and ecological injustice. Deriving from Paul F. Knitter, he promotes the idea of ecological economics. Ecological economics is concerned about the sustainability of the earth and envisions how human beings ought to live on planet earth.[17] The promotion of eco-justice through biodiversity is also important to bring justice closer to the poor.

Affirming that theology has the potential for an integral approach to reality, Felix Wilfred says there is an urgent need to rethink the narration of God in her relationship to the earth and the whole creation in such a way that the mystery of the divine is experienced immanently as present in nature and its dynamism. To have effective social justice and eco-justice, we need interreligious sharing and conversation since one religious vision can be corrective to another one, and there can be mutual enrichment in relating to the environment.[18]

Recognising that social justice and eco-justice are intertwined, Felix Wilfred says that a non-violent society and world is possible only when humans begin to live in harmony in their relationship with the earth and the entire creation.

The Ethics of Ecological Justice

In Christian tradition, the idea of justice is rooted in the very being of God and is an important aspect of God's community where all species relate with each other with justice. Here, love is an important force that guides us towards this justice. Without love, people are not pushed towards action. Love always gives passion to justice. Justice is love worked out.[19]

The biblical idea of justice with a greater sensitivity to the poor begins with the liberation of the oppressed slaves in Egypt, which is followed by establishing a covenant with them (Exod 22:21-24). Micah also summarises the law "to do justice, and to love kindness, and to walk humbly with your God" (Micah 6:8).

Prophets like Amos (Amos 2:6; 8:4-8; 5:11), Isaiah (Is 10:1-2) and Jeremiah (Jer 22: 13-17) talk always about justice and care for the poor. Likewise, Jesus who was a poor man from a poor part of Israel had a deep concern for the poor and their liberation (Luke 4:16-20). The early church was also concerned about the poor and emphasised equality and freedom (Gal 3:28). The early Christian community in Jerusalem (Acts 1-5), too, practised equality and sharing.[20] A Christian ethic towards poverty in the present times has to take into account ecological justice too.

In the context of climate change, ecological justice helps us address the ethical issues of the worst conditions of poverty, powerlessness, exploitation and environmental degradation. As far as ecological justice is concerned, the word 'ecological' points to the importance of other species and the word 'justice' points to a just order between the human and the natural world.[21] The ethics of ecological justice emphasises four moral norms: *sustainability, sufficiency, participation,* and *solidarity.*

Sustainability: Sustainability, as defined by James B. Martin-Schramm, is the long-range supply of sufficient resources to meet the basic human needs and the preservation of intact natural communities. It expresses a concern for future generations and the planet as a whole and emphasises that an acceptable quality of life for the present generation must not jeopardise the prospects for future generations. Sustainability means good stewardship, and it also challenges economic growth that harms the ecological system and ignores human needs and costs.[22]

Some of the biblical sources in relation to sustainability are Psalm 104, a hymn in praise of God's sustainability; and Psalm 145, which rejoices in the knowledge that God gives "them food in every season and satisfy the desire of every living thing." Schramm points out that the very responsibility of humans in this world is to assist God in maintaining the sustainability of God's creation. He says that the creation stories in Genesis 1:28 (referring to stewardship) and Genesis 2:15 ("till it and keep it") stress on humanity's role in being stewards of God's creation. He brings in other examples like the parable of the good steward in Luke 12:42 to explain how humanity is called to be earth's tenants and to serve the earth.

For Schramm, the covenant theme is also an important biblical and theological foundation for the norm of sustainability. The Noahic covenant, the covenant between God and all the living creation and all the flesh of the earth, demonstrates God's concern for biodiversity and the preservation of all species. More important is the Sinai covenant, where all the commandments are intended to sustain the life of the people of God in harmony with the well-being of the earth (Exod 20-24).[23]

The National Action Plan of Climate Change (NAPCC) initiated in 2008 in India has sustainability as its major focus. Its main purpose is to promote sustainable development in national development policies, taking climate change into consideration. It focuses on eight sectors to promote sustainability: agriculture, forestry, water, urban habitat, enhanced energy efficiency, solar energy, the Himalayan ecosystem, and education on climate change.[24]

Sufficiency: This would mean that "all forms of life are entitled to share in the goods of creation,"[25] which challenges unlimited consumption, holdings or inequitable distribution of earth's goods. It addresses the idea of sharing and equity. In the Bible, we see how God sends enough manna each day in the wilderness to sustain the community. The norm of sufficiency is an integral part of the jubilee legislation too. Schramm points out that these laws emphasise the stewardship of the land, care of animals and the poor, and a regular redistribution of wealth. In particular, the jubilee law stresses the need for the poor and wild animals to eat and for the earth to regenerate from the fields left fallow every seven years (Exod 23:11). All creatures are entitled to a sufficient amount of food to live.[26]

The idea of sufficiency emphasises the very idea of Jesus' saying "I came that you may live, and have it abundantly" (John 10:10). Jesus' ministry and his teaching were always about sharing life and possessions with people who are in need. Sharing was exemplified by the early church (Acts 1-5). This whole idea challenges the human-centred worldview of economic growth.

Participation: Participation stems from the affirmation to respect and include all forms of life in human decisions that affect the lives of all. According to Schramm, "Participation is concerned with empowerment and seeks to remove the obstacle to participating in decisions that affect lives."[27] The Genesis stories emphasise the need for humans to recognise the interests of God's creation and to act as good stewards of God. Prophets too have questioned and challenged the people in power against silencing the voices of the poor and the afflicted. Passages such as Mark 1:14-15, which speaks about Jesus' own emphasis on the kingdom or community of God, serve as a model for a participatory community. Participation at this point simply means how our selection of energy, resource systems, and the technologies we adopt are appropriate enough to not adversely affect the natural world and the poor. Schramm says that many of our decisions already have had negative consequences on human species and ecosystems. Beyond human reasoning, he says, it is important to see plants, animals, and their communities as having interests that we should respect. They have dignity and they also experience pleasure and pain. Participation calls us to give other species a voice.[28]

The Institute for Social and Environmental Transition–International (ISET-International), founded in 1997, has developed the Shared Learning Dialogue (SLD) process to address water issues in South Asia. The SLD process has been used in a number of projects and programmes in Bangladesh and Nepal. It aims to bring together available knowledge on climate change from a multitude of stakeholders at various levels, including local knowledge and perceptions. It is designed to ensure that vulnerable populations have the opportunity to participate in climate change assessment processes and to build their own adaptive capacity.[29]

Solidarity: It challenges individualism and calls everyone to join the cause of victims of ecological disaster and climate change. This is a call for the rich to listen to the poor and all of humanity to recognise the fundamental interdependence with the rest of nature. Schramm says that for solidarity, the virtues of humility, compassion, courage and generosity are important components.[30]

He says the biblical concept of *imago Dei* is the foundational concept for solidarity. This concept places humans not in a position over or apart from creation but in the same loving relationship with creation. Humans have to be in solidarity with the earth and other communities. The life of Jesus and his ministry is also a clear witness to compassionate solidarity. Jesus always was in solidarity with the poor, the marginalised, the suffering and the outcasts. Paul uses the metaphor "the body of Christ" to emphasise solidarity within the Christian community. In Christ, if one member suffers, all suffer together and if one member is honoured, all rejoice together (1 Cor 12:26).[31] This is compassionate solidarity. Schramm points to the cross as the central symbol to understand solidarity. "It points to a God who works in the world not in terms of power *over* but power *in, with,* and *under.*"[32]

The Climate Action Network–South Asia (CANSA) works to develop solidarity towards climate justice. This organisation has 60 non-governmental organisations (NGOs) from the six countries of South Asia as its members. CANSA works to reach to civil societies in all South Asian countries.[33] It works in organising, supporting and coordinating all its members in the South Asian countries to be one voice in challenging climate injustice. Churches everywhere too need to join such networks to fight against climate injustice.

Climate Justice

The victims of climate change are often the poor, indigenous, tribal people, Islanders, and earth-based communities. Their carbon emissions are very low, but they face the brunt of climate change. Christoph Stueckelberger, the founder of Globethics.net Foundation, says that "Who dies first?" and "Who pays how much?" are essentially questions of justice and that the ethical aspect of climate change should address the issue of justice and equity.[34] According to Stueckelberger, "Climate justice implies just and fair instruments, decisions, actions, sharing of the burden and accountability to prevent, mitigate and adapt to climate change."[35] The dimensions of climate justice he offers widens our discussion on ethics relating to climate change. For instance, by capability-related justice he means that every person or organisation has the duty to contribute to climate justice on the basis of their socio-economic, political, intellectual and spiritual capabilities. Needs-based justice, in his opinion, is about taking into account the basic rights and needs of every person or communities that are in dire need. Intergenerational justice is about sustainable use and fair distribution of resources, with the focus on reducing the ecological burden on the future generation. He also talks about participatory justice, procedural justice, and punitive justice.[36]

The report "Hiding behind the Poor" released by Greenpeace in 2007 clearly portrays how the excessive carbon emission of the rich and the middle class is impacting opportunities for the healthy living of the poor. This report emphasises the intergenerational (fairness between generations), international (fairness between states), and national (fairness between individuals) aspects of climate justice and equity.[37]

For instance, although Bangladesh, which has low carbon emissions, has always been the worst affected country in South Asia owing to climate change. Excessive flooding in July 2020 in Bangladesh affected more than 2.4 million people, including 1.3 million children. More than half a million (548,816) families lost their homes. This is at a time when the country's public health systems have been working hard to contain the spread of COVID-19.

In India, at around the same time, floods wreaked havoc, affecting some 2.4 million children alone. In Nepal, floods affected over 10,000 people—half of them children—in 20 districts and displaced 7,500 people.[38]

The impact of climate change on poor and innocent children in South Asian countries clearly shows how justice eludes the vulnerable. Rich nations have the capacity, economy and mechanisms to recover from climate disasters, but poor nations and people whose carbon footprints are comparatively lower pay the price.

A Neighbour-Love Ethic for Climate Change

Cynthia Moe-Lobeda considers "neighbour-love" as an important ethical principle in addressing the climate crisis. Neighbour love as such encompasses compassion and justice. Now neighbour-love adds a third ethical norm which is ecological: the earth's well-being. According to her, a neighbour-love ethics for climate change constitutes the following four principles:[39]

- Operating within the earth's economy (ecologically sustainable)

- Heeding environmental space and ecological debt (environmentally equitable)

- Prioritising human needs and the earth's needs over maximising profit and accumulating wealth (economically equitable)

- Challenging concentrated economic power and seeking to distribute economic power (democratic)

The first principle of ecological sustainability requires to situate human economies within the earth's economy. This is a challenge to move from the dependence of fossil fuel. As a result, says Moe-Lobeda, "the high value of over-consumption will shift to the values of sufficiency or frugality. The value of globally traded food products will convert to valuing local and regionally produced and traded goods. Disposable goods will give way to enduring, repaired, and reused goods."[40]

The next aspect of ecological sustainability is to address the concern of ecological debt and environmental footprint. These concerns involve how the Global North has plundered the ecological space of the Third World countries. Moe-Lobeda says that "ecological debt refers to the 'debt' owed by the countries of the Global North to the people of the Global South as a result of disproportionate greenhouse gas emissions and toxic waste dumping, other forms of ecological damage, and 500 years of resource plundering that have brought riches to the North at the expense of the South."[41] In this context, Moe-Lobeda points out how the "biblical notions of the Jubilee and Sabbath are integrally connected with the teachings of Jeremiah, Amos, Hosea, and other Hebrew prophets who denounce the rich for building their luxurious lives on goods stolen from the poor."[42]

The third aspect of this neighbour-love ethic is that of economic equity which involves prioritising human needs over profit maximisation. Moe-Lobeda points out the example of Coca-Cola company in India which spoiled the water and land of marginal farmers for their profit. Only changes in values, public policy and everyday practices can bring about a change in such a situation. According to Moe-Lobeda, "neighbour-love, along with much political-economic theory, suggests a different path. It is the societal decision that profit maximization and wealth accumulation will take a back seat to ecological sustainability and human need."[43]

The fourth aspect of the neighbour-love ethic that Moe-Lobeda proposes is that of economic democracy. Here she identifies the problem as that of concentrated corporate power in the context of a neoliberal global economy. She says the "power to make decisions regarding water, food, forests, mineral resources, food-processing lands, and more is increasingly in the hands of a few people who are accountable to no one except corporate shareholders…. This process subordinates *democracy* (rule by the people) to rule by the corporation."[44] Neighbour-love challenges this concentration of unaccountable economic power and favours policies and practices that guard against unchecked concentrations of economic power.[45]

Climate justice links human rights and development to achieve a human-centred approach, safeguarding the rights of the most vulnerable and sharing their burdens. Climate justice activism needs to be informed by clear analysis, data and lived experiences of people. Hence it confidently responds to science, economics and politics to design policies that include the concerns and voices of the people who are vulnerable to climate change.

Climate Change: Learning from Grassroots Social Movements

A review of the literature in the field of Christian ethics reveal that an engagement with the social realities has always been the subject matter of Christian ethics. However, this engagement lacks a political commitment. The vantage points of the grassroots communities and their social movements are not privileged in the mainstream Christian ethical discourses. As a result, we see these communities and their movements "added" and "represented" in our ethical discussions, without being able to contest and destabilise the dominant ethical discourses.

According to George Mathew Nalunnakkal, mainstream green theologies talk about ecology in general terms and cosmetic terms. Most often they give importance to recycling, but do not address the structural issues that cause the environmental crisis: capitalism and its model of development. His concept of "kenotic anthropocentrism" is a useful corrective in today's world of consumerism.[46] Kenotic anthropocentrism, according to him, is where we empty ourselves and serve creation by being tillers and keepers of creation.

George Zachariah, in his book *Alternatives Unincorporated: Earth Ethics from the Grassroots,* proposes a grassroots earth ethics with a theological methodology of "social movements as theological texts," which affirms the moral agency of the grassroots communities in creating a different world.[47] He affirms that theological and ethical praxis emerges in the crucible of subaltern politics to reclaim the moral agency of the people to realise their visions of liberation. He emphasises that social movements, as agents of counter-hegemonic praxis, are partakers in the salvific project of decolonisation where gospel is happening, hence becoming a *theandric* moment.[48] According to him, the story of Jonah and Nineveh is an important paradigm for us to believe and act towards a social *metanoia* (conversion) where God is at work in our midst, inviting people to turn and to repent.[49] Today social movements are akin to Jonah bringing us the message of repentance and at the same time providing us with ethical guidelines for a social *metanoia* and to live righteously in the presence of God.

Even as we strive together to flourish the movement of life in the context of climate change, climate justice ethics invites us to rethink our mainstream engagement with the climate crisis. The crisis that we face today is more than a change in the weather patterns. It is not nature's fury or wrath of God. Rather, it is the consequence of the prevailing socio-economic and ecological relations. Climate justice ethics enables us to look for alternative problematisations and radical political initiatives for a just recovery. Climate justice ethics provides us alternative ethical norms, principles and goals, drawn from the Scripture and tradition, that are life-affirming. The alternative norms and goals are informed by the struggles, ethics, politics and spirituality of the subaltern communities and the grassroots social movements, and they have the potential to redeem the earth.

Endnotes

[1] K. C. Abraham, *Transforming Vision: Theological–Methodological Paradigm Shifts,* (Tiruvalla: CSS, 2006).

[2] Ibid., 79.

[3] Ibid., 178-179.

[4] Economics deals with relationships of production, distribution, and consumption; Ecology is the comprehensive term for all the ecosystems of all that is living and non-living; and Ecumenics is used to describe the household of God, the church.

[5] K. C. Abraham, *Eco-Justice: A New Agenda for Church's Mission,* (Allahabad: Servisage, 2000), 36-37.

[6] K. C. Abraham, "A Theological Response to the Ecological Crisis," in *Ecotheology: Voices from South and North,* David G. Hallman, ed., (New York: WCC/Orbis books, 1994), 70.

[7] K.C. Abraham, *Transforming Vision: Theological–Methodological Paradigm Shifts,* Op.cit, 175-179.

[8] Ibid., 181.

[9] Ibid., 181-182.

[10] K.C. Abraham derives this idea from Andrew Linzey. p195.

[11] Ibid., 197 -198.

[12] Ibid., 207.

[13] Ibid., 214–216.

[14] Felix Wilfred, "Prophetic Ecotheology: The Need of the Hour," A paper presented at the symposium *Environmental Ethics and Pastoral Challenges,* in Mary Matha Major Seminary, Mulayam, Kerala, on 9 August 2013, 3-4.

[15] Ibid., 7-8.

[16] Felix Wilfred derives this idea of "Kinship" from Cf. John Hart. Kinship expresses the interdependence of humans and nature. St. Francis of Assisi, who dealt with birds, fishes and animals in a relationship of kinship, could address the sun as brother and the moon as sister. Felix Wilfred, *Asian Public*

Theology: Critical Concerns in Challenging times, (Delhi: ISPCK, 2010), 157.

[17] Felix Wilfred, Felix Wilfred, *Asian Public Theology: Critical Concerns in Challenging times,* Op.cit., 160.

[18] Ibid., 162–163.

[19] Ibid.,

[20] James B. Martin-Schramm, *Climate Justice: Ethics, Energy, And Public Policy,* (Fortress Press: Minneapolis, 2010), 37.

[21] Ibid., 28.

[22] Ibid., 28.

[23] Ibid., 30.

[24] https://www.researchgate.net/publication/279956976_Environmental_Justice_in_India, accessed on 10 Feb 2020.

[25] James B. Martin-Schramm, 30.

[26] Ibid., 31.

[27] Ibid., 33.

[28] Ibid., 35.

[29] https://www-cdn.oxfam.org/s3fs-public/file_attachments/rr-climate-change-adaptation-south-asia-161111-en_3.pdf, Accessed on 10 Feb 2020.

[30] James B. Martin-Schramm, 35.

[31] Ibid., 36.

[32] Ibid., 36.

[33] http://www.climatenetwork.org/profile/member/climate-action-network-south-asia-cansa, Accessed on 15 Feb 2020.

[34] Christoph Stueckelberger, "Who Dies First? Who is Sacrificed First? Ethical Aspects of Climate Justice," in *God, Creation and Climate Change: Spiritual and Ethical Perspectives,* edited by Karen L. Bloomquist, Geneva: LWF Studies, 2009, 201.

[35] Ibid., 201.

[36] Cynthia Moe-Lobeda., 203.

[37] https://mronline.org/2019/10/11/climate-justice-in-india-a-critical-overview/, Accessed on 10 Feb 2020.

[38] https://www.unicef.org/press-releases/millions-children-affected-devastating-flooding-south-asia-many-more-risk-covid-19.

[39] Cynthia Moe-Lobeda, 231.

[40] Ibid., 204.

41 Ibid., 210.

42 Ibid., 213.

43 Ibid., 219.

44 Ibid., 227.

45 George Mathew Nalunnakkal, *Green Liberation*, 227.

46 Ibid., 261.

47 He proposes this idea using Narmada Bachao Andolan. For him, subaltern oppositional gaze, mediations with social theories and engagement with religious sources, alternative political vision and celebration of life in resistance and recreation are the cartographies of this grassroots earth ethics. For him, the struggles of subaltern communities like Dalits and Adivasis are the sources for experiencing God's politics of liberation. See George Zachariah, *Alternatives Unincorporated: Earth Ethics from the Grass Roots*, (London: Equinox, 2011), 98 - 120.

48 George Mathew Nalunnakkal, 98.

49 George Zachariah, "Discerning the Times: A Spirituality of Resistance and Alternatives," in *God Creation and Climate Change: Spiritual and Ethical Perspectives*, edited by Karen L. Bloomquist, (Geneva: LWF Studies,2009), 90-91.

Chapter 6

Church and Climate Change

The church is founded on the redemptive and salvific life of Christ. And the church is called to live as a witness to God's salvific work through Jesus Christ. The context of climate change has widened our theological understanding of salvation for all, which includes the earth and the cosmos. And most importantly, the church is called to be the presence of God's resistance to create the reign of God in this world. In which case the church has to play a major role in challenging the forces causing climate change and to envision itself as a place to experience God's love and compassion and promote climate justice. In a context where climate change causes hopelessness and nihilism, churches can be a place that instill hope to renew the world. Christians should believe that the world has to be made anew; for this the church should consider as its purpose the redemption of the earth along with human beings. This section focuses on how the church has to redefine its role and responsibilities, worship and liturgy, preaching, spiritual practices such as fasting, and prophetic ministry in the context of climate change. The chapter also offers guidelines for practical applications in churches for climate justice.

Reimagining the Marks of the Church in the Context of Climate Crisis

In the discussions on ecclesiology, we always talk about the marks of the church. In the context of the climate crisis, it is important for us to reimagine the marks of the church to transform the church into a community that helps life to flourish in the midst of death and destruction. Jim Antal, a climate activist and public theologian, identifies the essential marks of the church in the context of climate crisis as follows. First of all, the church has to remind itself of its role as the keeper of continuity. It is incumbent on the church as keepers of the community to uphold the God-given task to protect God's creation for which it has to think strongly about cosmic salvation more than personal salvation. The church should embrace and teach more about spiritual progress than material progress. That entails a will to challenge capitalist forces causing climate change, change personal lifestyles to reduce carbon emission, and to be convinced that our interdependence with God is based on the interdependence with creation. The church has to stand with people who are engaged in non-violent struggles to protect the earth and the vulnerable communities. Most importantly, churches should network with other churches and work together to celebrate our diverse gifts.[1]

Worship and Liturgy

Worship is always two-dimensional. It involves reflecting on God and our faithful response to work according to God's will in this world. Worship in the context of climate crisis helps us to reflect on the presence of God in all created beings and realise God's purpose for the sustenance and well-being of the whole cosmos. With this realisation, we have to reorient ourselves in restoring our distorted relationship and reconcile ourselves with

God and nature. This reconciled relationship will also challenge ourselves to stand against injustices, oppression, negligence and discrimination against the earth and all its inhabitants. Hence worship becomes a subversive act which helps us in envisioning an alternative lifestyle guided by our faith to live with the created order.

Many churches have sought to respond to climate crisis by instituting a movement to observe a liturgical season of creation. *The Season of Creation: A Preaching Commentary* is the outcome of such an initiative involving scholars who bring about the connections between biblical scholarship, ecological theology, liturgy and homiletics. The book is a comprehensive resource for preaching and leading worship and has theological and practical introductions to help preachers and worship leaders guide their congregations to have a deeper connect with our imperiled planet. With regard to worship it says:

> Worship can be subversive of the culture and an expression of countercultural thinking and acting. Worship can lead us to counter the consumer mentality and practices of our time that treat people and Earth as commodities to be exploited. It can lead us to advocate for public policies and laws that foster the love of neighbor and care for creation. At the same time, our reorientation in worship may lead us to affirm many movements and actions in our culture around us that further the kinds of values and behaviors fostered by Christian ways of being in the world.
>
> By drawing us into a reorientation of relationships, worship is meant to give us a taste of new creation—creation redeemed and reconciled.[2]

How can we bring into practice a radical reorientation to God and the earth through our worship is a practical question churches may tend to ask. *The Season of Creation* gives us theological guidance and insights into how we can make use of the seasons of the church year—Advent, Christmas, Epiphany, Lent, Easter, Pentecost, etc.—to address climate change and renewal of the earth.

In addition to this, the book provides several practical guidelines. For instance, green and flowering plants can always decorate our sanctuaries. Worship at certain times can be conducted outside the church walls. Earth-friendly elements such as locally made candles, bread and wine made from organically cultivated wheat or grape, juice/wine, recyclable papers, earthen-based worship vessels, and so on, can be part of the worship.[3] Our worships cannot reorient ourselves to God without our remembering and praying for/with nature.

> For us to be truly reoriented by God in our worship, we should incorporate a love for, a celebration of, concern for, prayer for, and a commitment to care for all creation into every dimension of our worship experience. Just as we cannot imagine worship without praise of God and expressions of love for others, especially those in need, so, too, we should not be able to imagine worship without expressions of our love for and our commitment to God's creation.[4]

Most mainline churches are liturgically based with regard to worship. Though the Pentecostal or Free churches may not follow a written or structured liturgy, they still have the expressions of the liturgy in their worship based on their theological affirmations. The elements of worship, whether liturgical or non-liturgical, can be easily adapted to worship God with all creation. *The Season of Creation* also provides important theological articulations of how these liturgical elements of worship can be extended to include nature as part of the worship. The invocation in our worship can address "God as the God of all creation."

Churches that use the Gloria can invite the congregation to join with the communion of all creation.

Confession and absolution is an important aspect of worship which helps us to confess our sins against God's creation and to restore our relationship with God's creation. Scripture readings ought to help us recognise the voice of creation and how God uses creation for the salvific mission. In our prayers and offerings, our thanksgiving can focus on all the ecological gifts and also commit ourselves to be in solidarity with the victims of climate change. The Eucharist, one of the most important sacraments of the church where bread and wine are used, will always remind ourselves of our communion with God's presence in creation. Finally, our commission and blessing can always emphasise on sending believers for ministry to earth.[5]

The church should also think about "Liturgy in the Street." Public liturgy means our participation with people who protest against ecological destruction through our presence and prayers. It is also an opportunity to join with people of other religious faiths to share our faith resources for a more united struggle. Songs, prayers, reading of scriptures and preaching on this occasion can be made relevant to widen our Christian commitment to God's creation and for the church to express its faith in the street.

Benjamin Stewart, in his article "Worship Without Walls," emphasises the significance of worship and rituals in public. He argues that rituals in public have to be seen as a form of pilgrimage. According to him, this pilgrim approach does not strictly divide people into believers and non-believers but regards all people as potential seekers after the most true of the world. And this approach is very important in this religiously pluralistic context.[6]

Prophetic Preaching on Climate Change

Preaching is an important aspect in the church to encourage and help the congregation to understand their misconceptions, fears and complacency regarding climate change. Preaching creates a condition in which people can face the reality of climate change and respond to God's call to take action to protect God's creation and also extend solidarity with people who are already engaged in this work. Jim Antal offers ten considerations for preaching on climate change.[7]

1. **Do not start with science, with fear, or with headlines.** Instead begin by asking yourself: what is the collective story of the congregation? What is their social identity? What are their common deeply held values? And then, how are these values challenged by the disorder and discontinuity brought about by climate change?

2. **It is good to acknowledge ambivalence.** Do not assume that everyone knows what you know; even if they do know, do not assume that they care for it the same way you do.

3. **Cite one fact, not a bunch of science.** It may not be very helpful sometimes to explain a lot of scientific details and reports. Try to share one powerful fact from a trusted messenger. What affects most people in the sermon are not data but values, moral narratives, and imagery.

4.   **Keep it simple.** People need to be told facts without getting too much into the complexity of climate science or ideological debates.

5. **Do what the Golden Rule does.** Provide a narrative that invites people to recognise our *shared* humanity, reminding facts like all creatures on the planet breath

the same air. Regarding the challenge of climate change, no one has an alibi—we are literally all in this together.

6. **Embrace Jesus' most frequent admonition, "Fear not."** Climate change encourages fear, denial and unwillingness to accept our responsibility. It is important to derive insights from Jesus on how we can challenge fear and act courageously in our present context. It is important to ask in the context of a world disordered by unchecked fear, greed and growth, what is God's good news? Preach on that.

7. **Lead your congregation to recognise that the time to act is NOW.** It is challenging to prompt action on an issue that may not seem to pose an immediate threat. When extreme storms happen, it is important to involve in immediate disaster reliefs and also to renew our commitment to political advocacy for sane and sensible climate policies.

8. **Make it local, personal, immediate and abrupt.** This is because people are not conditioned to deal with threats that are distant or abstract.

9. **Claim your moral leadership as a member of the clergy.** For the most part, congregations respect and trust the clergy, and research confirms that audiences are more receptive to messages from someone they respect and trust.

10. **Lead more faithful and hopeful lives.** As leaders of faith communities, it is up to us to offer new ways to live faithfully and hopefully in a world which is moving discontinuously from the world in which we were born.

Carbon Fast and Lent

Carbon fasting was originally developed by the Church of England in 2008. Since then, it has been adopted by congregations of many different denominations around the world as a faith response by individuals and communities to turn away from actions that release carbon into the atmosphere. Carbon fasting is an effective spiritual way to reduce our carbon emissions as a faith response to the climate crisis. This faith practice is also about following a way of life that honours God's call to love the whole world and care for the most vulnerable.[8]

Anglicans have been at the lead of a move to follow carbon fasting during Lent. Six dioceses in southwest England developed resources for individual people and church and school communities to observe carbon fasting.[9] In 2014, carbon fasting became a part of their Lenten spiritual devotion and helped them discover the financial benefits of stewarding resources. They undertook a specific challenge to reduce energy consumption by 40 per cent for the 40 days of Lent. The focus was on using water and energy wisely and be conscious about carbon consumption.

Similarly, in 2017, the then Moderator of the Church of South India, Most Rev. Thomas K. Oommen, sent a path-breaking letter inviting churches to involve in carbon fasting during Lent. In this letter, he points out the reason for carbon fasting as an important aspect of Christian response to the present climate crisis in India as follows:[10]

> The Bible urges us "Go into all the world and proclaim the good news to the whole creation." How will we proclaim the good news to the whole creation when there is no water to drink? As per scientific predictions, by 2070, one human being will have only two glasses of water to drink per day. By 2035, Ganga, Brahmaputra, and Indus rivers will disappear. Yes, Climate Change is going to affect all creations of God. A scorching

heatwave in India has killed more than 1,500 people in 2015 as temperatures soared above 47⁰C. Southern Andhra Pradesh and Telangana states are the worst-hit regions with more than 1,100 deaths, mainly caused by extreme dehydration and heatstroke. The situation in northern India is not too different, with Kanpur, in Uttar Pradesh state, registering a record high temperature of 47 ⁰C. In 2016, three hundred and thirty million people, more than a quarter of India's population, were hit by drought. The whole creation has been groaning for water due to desertification, which is an irreversible process. The migration of poor people and wild animals is now common.

A carbon fast is a challenge for us to look at our daily actions, to reflect on how they impact on the environment. It challenges us to take some small steps—some of which will reduce our carbon dioxide output while others will help the environment— for a more sustainable world. In the process, we may come to rediscover a different relationship with God, with His Creation and with one another. Most of the CSI Congregations belong to the communities that are vulnerable to Climate Change. We create awareness on "Climate Justice" at the congregational level in these dioceses. Further, re-read the Bible and reaffirm our faith from the perspective of Climate Refugees. We inspire the congregations to discern climate justice as an integral part of the church's public witness today. We hope that the congregations would be equipped to involve in saving creations whose life and livelihood are under threat.

Moreover, the CSI also devised a plan for the churches to observe carbon fasting based on various themes for each week. These included simplifying our lives; focusing on trees and forests; conserving electricity and reducing emissions; conserving water; and adopting the "reduce, reuse, recycle" policy.

The Mar Thoma Church, too, took an initiative in observing environmental Sunday to urge the faithful to stay away from "eco-sins." In his circular, the Metropolitan of the Mar Thoma Church, Joseph Mar Thoma, expanded the idea of sin as that which "is not merely embracing evil; misuse of nature that God declared as good also amounts to the denial of God."[11] The main idea behind this is to preserve the natural resources for the future generation which is an important eco-justice mission of the Church. The Metropolitan urged the churches to preach the scriptural message, "The earth is the Lord's and all that is in it, the world and those who live in it" (Ps 24:1).

Philipose Mar Chrysostom, the emeritus Metropolitan of the Mar Thoma Church, too urged the church towards carbon fasting. He asked the congregation to switch off electrical equipment when not in use and to remove one electric bulb and live without it for the 50 days of Lent as a period of penitence.[12] This was a call for the faithful to commit to reduce carbon emissions during the season of Lent.

Carbon Tithe

The Quaker community in the United States in several places has initiated a practice of carbon tithe. This is about committing themselves to collect a carbon tax for the level of carbon emission they contribute. In other words, to pay tax according to each one's carbon footprint—the amount of carbon dioxide or other carbon compounds emitted due to the consumption of fossil fuels by a particular person or group. This practice emerges from the recognition that coming forward for a voluntary carbon tax affirms the commitment to live with responsibility and to care for creation.[13]

A Quaker group, Mount Toby's Voluntary Carbon Tax Witness group, explains the basic idea of carbon tithe as follows:[14]

1. A group of interested people agrees to "tax" themselves a percentage of their spending on fossil fuels for their vehicles, their electricity (if applicable), their home

heating, and their air travel. Each person makes his or her own commitment. Names, but not amounts, are publicised.

2. They send the money to a dedicated sub-account in their congregation.

3. Every quarter they decide where to gift the money such collected (emissions reduction projects, climate justice, adaptation projects, response efforts, etc.).

4. They share their results with the congregation and beyond.

These committed Quaker groups are also multifaith in nature and encourage other groups to adopt voluntary taxation. In their gathering and fellowship time, they have very detailed conversations about climate change and climate action. These gatherings also allow participants to analyse how much fuel they use for their needs. Carbon tithing in this context makes the participants feel empowered as they find a chance to practically do something about their contribution to climate change rather than living with guilt.[15]

The money that is collected goes to action groups or organisations that are involved in directly reducing carbon emissions. These include organisations involved in the installation of solar panels or those committed to greenhouse gas reduction programmes. The money is also used to buy carbon offsets or for educational outreach.

Carbon tithing can be a practice that Indian churches can follow. The money collected can be sent to grassroots organisations and support communities that are affected by climate disasters. Rich Christian congregations, especially, can contribute a sum to support congregations whose lifestyle contributes less to carbon emission. It can also be utilised to support alternative energy use for a church and individual houses. While carbon fasting helps us to commit ourselves to reduce carbon emission, carbon tithing will help us to commit ourselves to contribute financially as an act of repentance and join in the process of alternative living.

Climate Prophetism

To be a prophet requires great courage and commitment to challenge powerful forces and to pronounce God's ways of justice. Today there are several young people who are fighting like prophets against climate change in South Asia. Their work should be an inspiration for the Indian churches.

Smriti is a 19-year-old climate activist from Bangladesh where severe flooding, storms, cyclones and droughts are a recurrent phenomena. She works with YouthNet for Climate Justice, which is a UNICEF-supported network of many young people who are committed to fight against climate change. Her concern especially has been on how climate change increases child marriages and affects almost three million children in Bangladesh. Because of climate change and increasing poverty, many parents force their daughters to get married soon. Smriti has been visiting many parents and children in schools, creating awareness about children's rights and about reducing child marriages. She has been constantly talking to government officials and key decision-makers regarding climate change and the struggles of young brides.[16]

Kyaw Ye Htet, who is a social science student in Yangon, Myanmar, has been organising climate strikes from 2018, inspiring several people to join and express their voices towards climate injustice. Myanmar has been very vulnerable to the impact of climate change and many in the country think that climatic disorder is natural. Kyaw Ye Htet's aim is to change their attitude, raise awareness and encourage people to join the "Climate Strike Myanmar" group. He has also been raising voice against dam projects and coal-related energy projects in his area.[17]

Ili Nadiah Dzulfakar, an environmental sciences student in Malaysia, is the co-founder of Klima Action Malaysia (KAMY). This group joins with the country's indigenous groups that are battling big business for their forest lands. This is an attempt to get the indigenous voices heard in climate change protests. This group has been working hard to push the government towards political commitment. There has been a lot of backlash for Nadiah and her group in Malaysia. Some people completely deny climate change and others do not like to challenge the big corporations. Nevertheless, the activist is very much encouraged that their group has been able to push more Malaysians to think about climate solutions.[18]

Marinel Ubaldo, aged 22, is a climate activist in the Philippines. She survived Super Typhoon Haiyan, which killed more than 6,300 people in 2013, including some of her relatives and friends. Since then Ubaldo has been working on climate change issues in her coastal home of Matarinao where the typhoon struck. She also has been raising voices against oil and gas corporations in Manila. Hers is a prophetic voice in challenging fossil fuel firms that violate human rights concerns.[19]

Licypriya Kangujam is an eight-year-old climate activist from India. She has been challenging world leaders and global organisations to take immediate action to combat climate change. She wants children to have a better future and a cleaner planet.

She has been raising her voice against the Indian government with regard to air pollution and the country's climate policies. She wants fossil fuels and carbon emissions to be regulated. Her area of focus is on climate justice and climate education. She has been strongly advocating for including lessons about climate change in the school curricula. She envisions every student in India planting 10 trees so that there will be more trees in the country.[20]

In an article titled "Two Generations, one prophetic call for climate justice," The National Catholic Reporter online narrates the meeting of Pope Francis and Greta Thunberg in the Vatican on 17 April 2019. The meeting was described as "an encounter between two prophets whose moral clarity will lead us out of the climate crisis."[21] Pope Francis 82 years old, "with a wreath of white hair and an often-delighted smile," sees action on climate change as a way to protect vulnerable people as an essential part of his Christian vocation. At 16-years-old, "with her hair in a braid," Greta sees action on climate change as a fight that is essential to her future, a fight for her very survival. Pope Francis recognises that older generations have a responsibility to solve the challenges they have created. Greta recognises that younger generations have an opportunity to solve the challenges they have inherited. Greta recently told the European Parliament that "the house is on fire." Francis has written that "the earth, our home, is beginning to look more and more like an immense pile of filth."[22]

The Christian Century reported how Thunberg's speech at the United Nations Climate Action Summit was very similar to that of the biblical prophet who disturbs us:[23]

> Speaking at the United Nations Climate Action Summit last month, 16-year-old activist Greta Thunberg did not attempt to

ingratiate herself with world leaders. Like a biblical prophet, she was angry and her indictment of those in power was withering: "People are suffering. People are dying. Entire ecosystems are collapsing. We are in the beginning of a mass extinction, and all you can talk about is money and fairy tales of eternal economic growth."

Like a true prophet, Thunberg offered no false hope. Summarizing climate science in a few sentences, she warned that even cutting world carbon emissions in half in ten years— the most ambitious proposal on the global agenda—has only a 50 per cent chance of keeping temperature rise below 1.5 degrees Celsius. "Fifty per cent may be acceptable to you. But those numbers do not include tipping points, most feedback loops, additional warming hidden by toxic air pollution, or the aspects of equity and climate justice. They also rely on my generation sucking hundreds of billions of tons of your CO_2 out of the air with technologies that barely exist. So a 50 per cent risk is simply not acceptable to us—we who have to live with the consequences."

Pope Francis's message for the World Day of Prayer for Care of Creation on 1 September 2009 emphasised how our season of prayer should be focused on challenging climate actions. In his message, the Pope said:[24]

This too is a season for undertaking prophetic actions. Many young people all over the world are making their voices heard and calling for courageous decisions…. Our prayers and appeals are directed first at raising the awareness of political and civil leaders. The words that Moses proclaimed to the people as a kind of spiritual testament at the threshold of the Promised Land come to mind: "Therefore choose life, that you and your descendants may live" (Dt 3:19). We can apply those prophetic words to ourselves and the situation of our earth. Let us choose life! Let us say "no" to consumerist greed and the illusion of omnipotence, for these are the ways of death. Let us inaugurate farsighted processes involving responsible sacrifices today for the sake of sure prospects for life tomorrow. Let us not give in to the perverse logic of quick profit, but look instead to our common future!

Prophetic young people like Thunberg who challenge countries and corporates causing climate change have a very daunting task.

The very recent gathering in January 2020 of five young people in the Arctic Basecamp in Davos, Switzerland, as activists of climate change shows young people can be prophets of change. Kaime Silvestre, 23, from Brazil, who was one among them, said: "I'm from Brazil, and I'm from the Amazon region, but what is happening in the Arctic is affecting all of us. I'm here to put pressure on our global leaders to protect the Arctic."[25] These voices of courage and hope of several young people around the world are challenging and inspiring us to work towards protecting the earth and to avert more climate crises in the future.

The South Asian churches today are called to support and align with such young prophets to stand against forces causing the climate crisis.

Divestment and Fossil-Free Churches

Churches in the West and developed countries have the history of investing in various business companies, especially in fossil fuel companies, a phenomenon unknown to churches in Third World countries. Divestment as a concept in the West is not a new idea. Organisations divested from business in South Africa when its government supported apartheid. By the mid-1980s, 155 campuses, including some of the most famous in the world, had divested from companies doing business in South Africa. As many as 26 state governments, 22 countries and 90 cities took their money from multinationals that did business in the country. This act of divestment was to ensure democracy and equality.[26]

The most recent and powerful attempts to reduce climate change are to exert social, political and economic pressure on institutions for divestment of assets including stocks, bonds and other financial instruments connected to companies involved in extracting fossil fuels.

Fossil fuel divestment campaigns emerged in the United States where students started urging their administrations to divest from the fossil fuel industry in 2010. This campaign soon spread and several churches and Christian organisations are beginning to divest from fossil fuel investments.

Bill McKibben, a prominent climate activist and writer, was one of the persons to strongly advocate for organisations to divest their investment in fossil fuel companies. The goal of the divestment movement was to increase public awareness on two realities. From a practical perspective, 80 per cent of the known fossil fuel reserves (worth about $20 trillion) would need to be left in the ground. From a moral perspective, it challenges the fuel companies to think about the practices of making money for their investors by wrecking the earth.[27]

In 2013, the United Church of Christ became the first entity to implement divestment in the United States. It also passed a resolution to make its church buildings carbon neutral.[28] Following this, many churches and seminaries like the Union Theological Seminary in New York and the Lutheran School of Theology at Chicago divested its investment from fossil fuel companies in the US.

The divestment campaign in recent times aims to urge fossil fuel companies to adopt policies that support the 2015 Paris Agreement on climate change, which calls for action to keep the rise in global temperatures below 2 °C from pre-industrial levels. It is important to note that the largest group to announce divestment is 40 Catholic organisations in October 2017. It is believed that Catholic organisations became increasingly active on climate change concerns following Pope Francis' 2015 encyclical, *Laudato si'*, which calls on Catholics to live more sustainably.

Several organisations have been campaigning and promoting fossil fuel divestment. Operation Noah is a Christian organisation that began campaigning for divestment of fossil fuel in 2004. It is involved in sensitising churches and individual members of the Christian community to agree to fossil fuel divestment, debate the ethics of investing in fossil fuel firms, and use their resources to support the development of clean alternatives to fossil fuels such as solar and wind power.[29]

On Epiphany day on 6 January 2020, as many as 20 churches, dioceses, religious orders and Christian institutions in the United Kingdom announced their divestment from fossil fuel companies. They joined the growing "Fossil Free" divestment movement, where faith institutions make up 29 per cent of the divesting organisations, the greatest proportion of divestment commitments globally. The institutions proclaiming their divestment as part of the joint announcement included two Catholic Dioceses (Middlesbrough and Lancaster), the United Reformed Church's Synod of Wales and South Western Synod, several local churches and two Catholic religious orders.[30]

During this occasion, Bishop Terry Drainey, the Bishop of Middlesbrough, said:

> With growing awareness of people's concerns for the care of our common home, supported by the Trustees and Council of Priests of the Diocese, and after a thorough scrutiny of diocesan investments and with support from Operation Noah, the Diocese

of Middlesbrough has decided that now is the time to divest from fossil fuels. The evidence and the urgency of the climate crisis are all around us. However, as Pope Francis points out very clearly in his Encyclical Letter on The Care of Our Common Home, Laudato Si', nothing will succeed if we do not begin with personal conversion, a change in lifestyle, a change of mindset.

Reverend Simon Walkling, Moderator of the United Reformed Church Synod of Wales, said:

> We have decided to divest from fossil fuels in response to the growing climate crisis. This is part of the Church's desire to respond to the climate emergency and act for the future of our children and grandchildren, as well as the many people around the world who are already experiencing the devastating impacts of climate change.

James Buchanan, Bright Now Campaign Manager for Operation Noah, responded:

> It is wonderful news that so many Christian organizations have made the decision to divest from fossil fuels, including the first Catholic dioceses in the UK…. We hope many more Churches and other institutions will join them out of concern for those most affected by the climate crisis—especially people living in the world's poorest communities.

In the South Asian context, we definitely have many faithful believers who are rich and invest in fossil-based companies. It is time for them to rethink their Christian calling to make their investments in green-based technologies.

Practising New Forms of Christian Living

Christianity was born when several people committed themselves to a new life informed by the principles of Jesus Christ. This alternative lifestyle was about compassion to the underprivileged, justice, inclusivity, and a vision for life for all. We are now in a *kairos* moment, where we are called as a church to commit ourselves to Christian living that promotes justice to the victims of climate change. The following are some of the suggestions for a new Christian living.

The churches in South Asia should continuously urge their congregations to lead a sustainable lifestyle which is based on low carbon consumption that reflects their calling for "climate stewardship." Such commitment from individuals and congregations will witness to the world the foretaste of God's reign. The concept of "green congregations" will enable members of churches to commit themselves to energy saving technologies for their houses and church buildings.

Worship has an important role in making the congregation realise that they are worshipping the Creator and that creation is also groaning towards redemption. Our liturgies and prayers should have components addressing climate change issues and our lectionaries should incorporate ecological texts. Eco-hermeneutics should be effectively employed in our preaching to educate the congregation towards climate concerns. Sunday school lessons too should incorporate in them theological and prophetic teachings on climate justice and value for God's creation.

Harnessing the knowledge of professionals in social sciences, humanities, engineering, technology and other areas of expertise will help churches to think from climate change perspectives. Church boards and departments that have dedicated themselves for working towards climate change should always be in touch with the congregation and effectively engage them in climate mission work.

Churches should also extend great support to organic farming. Churches can open their spaces to even sell such produce.

Churches in South Asia should always be ready to partner with social movements and organisations that raise their voices against climate injustice. They should always extend their solidarity with people's movements and participate in their protests and struggles. This is where the church can live its public witness.

Besides, people with commitment should be identified, equipped and supported for prophetic ministry focusing on the environment. This should also involve encouraging activists and groups who courageously challenge the socio-economic practices that cause climate change.

South Asian churches should also continuously voice their concerns nationally and internationally, advocating for alternative, cleaner energy resources and low-carbon development as per international climate protocols. Churches should always be grassroots churches, giving priority to the concerns of Dalits, Adivasis and other subaltern groups who live and work closely with nature. Also, churches should support them in both adaptation and mitigation strategies to combat climate change.

The church should be a place of shelter for victims of climate change and should be ready to donate generously for disaster management and relief. Finally, the church should be a "church for all" where the whole created order lives its abundant life without greed but with love and justice in the presence of God.

Endnotes

[1] This is a summary of the Marks of the Church given by Jim Antal. For more on this read Jim Antal, *Climate Church, Climate World: How People of Faith must Work for Change,* (New York: Rowman & Littlefield, 2018), 65-78.

[2] Norman C. Habel, David Rhoads, and H. Paul Santmire (eds.), *The Season of Creation: A Preaching Commentary,* (Minneapolis: Fortress Press, 2011), 21.

[3] Ibid., 23.

[4] Ibid., 23.

[5] Ibid., 24-31.

[6] Benjamin M. Stewart, "Worship Without Walls," https://www.christiancentury.org/article/2012-09/worship-without-walls, accessed on 10 Jan 2020.

[7] Jim Antal, *Climate Church, Climate World: How People of Faith must work for change,* (New York: Rowman& LittleField, 2018), 132-134. Antal derives these considerations from two books *Don't even Think About It: Why our Brains are Wired to Ignore Climate Change* and *Let's Talk Faith and Climate: Communication for Faith Leaders in 2016.*

[8] http://www.ecofaithrecovery.org/carbonfast/, accessed on 10 Jan 2020.

[9] https://www.arrcc.org.au/carbon_fast_for_lent, accessed on 10 Jan 2020.

[10] https://www.ecocongregationscotland.org/news/moderator-of-church-of-south-india-encourages-christians-to-carbon-fast-for-lent/, accessed on 10 Jan 2020.

[11] https://www.thehindu.com/news/cities/Kochi/it-is-a-sin-not-to-be-green-says-churchs-new-teaching/article4740360.ece, accessed on 10 Jan 2020.

[12] Ibid.,

[13] https://ptquaker.org/wp/wp-content/uploads/2016/11/Voluntary-Carbon-Tithe-Program.pdf, Accessed on 10 Jan 2020.

[14] Quakers often use the word *witness* to indicate that they are choosing to live out their faith.

[15] https://paipl.us/tag/carbon-tax/, accessed on 10 Jan 2020.

[16] https://www.unicef.org/rosa/stories/raising-voices-climate-change-bangladesh, accessed on 20 Jan 2020.

[17] https://thediplomat.com/2019/10/the-young-activists-fighting-southeast-asias-climate-crisis/, accessed on 20 Jan 2020.

18 https://thediplomat.com/2019/10/the-young-activists-fighting-southeast-asias-climate-crisis/, accessed on 20 Jan 2020.

19 Ibid.,

20 https://www.globalcitizen.org/en/content/youth-climate-activist-cleaning-up-india/, accessed on 5 Feb 2020.

21 https://www.ncronline.org/news/earthbeat/two-generations-one-prophetic-call-climate-justice, accessed on 5 Feb 2020.

22 https://www.ncronline.org/news/earthbeat/two-generations-one-prophetic-call-climate-justice, accessed on 5 Feb 2020.

23 https://www.christiancentury.org/article/editors/greta-thunberg-s-prophetic-speech-un-climate-action-summit, accessed on 5 Feb 2020.

24 https://catholicclimatemovement.global/a-season-for-undertaking-prophetic-action/, accessed on 10 Jan 2020.

25 https://www.rollingstone.com/politics/politics-features/davos-climate-change-roundtable-youth-activists-941166/, accessed on 20 Jan 2020.

26 https://gofossilfree.org/divestment/what-is-fossil-fuel-divestment/, accessed on 20 Jan 2020.

27 Jim Antal, 146.

28 https://www.mnn.com/money/sustainable-business-practices/stories/united-church-of-christ-becomes-first-church-to-divest, accessed on 20 Jan 2020.

29 https://www.mnn.com/money/sustainable-business-practices/stories/united-church-of-christ-becomes-first-church-to-divest, accessed on 20 Jan 2020.

30 https://operationnoah.org/news-events/news/press-release-20-christian-institutions-divest-from-fossil-fuels/ accessed on 20 Jan 2020.

"Come out of Her":
A Call to Resistance against Empire
Revelation 18

Climate change due to carbon emissions can be attributed to human greed and the exploitative capitalist economic system that has colonised the ecosystems of the poor in this world. People in India and many South Asian countries are victims of this "economic omnipotence" of empires. One of the main challenges for the church is to prophetically call out these empires and the lifestyle they promote. In this context, the Book of Revelation serves as a prophetic subversive literature which helps us craft a "theology of resistance." This Bible study is an attempt to gather insights and inspiration to deepen our commitment to engage in climate justice ministries that seek to destabilise the empires of our times.

Book of Revelation: A Manual for Resistance

The Book of Revelation has been identified by many scholars as a book of resistance against the Roman Empire. Chapter 18 offers a strong critique of the Roman Empire. As Pablo Richard observes, this chapter invites us to resist, to refuse to participate, and to create alternatives to the imperial order.[1]

Eugene Boring identifies four major issues in Rome that is equated with Babylon in Revelation. One, the idolatrous and blasphemous worship offered and encouraged by Rome, especially the emperor cult (18:3); two, the violence perpetrated by Rome, especially against Jews and Christians (18:24); three, Rome's blasphemous self-glorification (18:7); and four, Roman wealth—the massive use of economic and commercial language (18:3; 11-19, 23).[2] "Coming out" here means to reject the legitimacy claims of the empire.

Today climate change is caused by the exploitative economic practices of the highly developed and industrialised nations. In order to protect the earth and to reduce climatic changes we are invited to be communities of resistance, to resist the dominaton of empires and to come out of such exploitative economic practices.

Revelation 18 begins with the pronunciation of the end of the Empire, challenging the omnipresence and the omnipotence of the Roman Empire and its false promises, and the deceiving nature of its economic claims. Most importantly, by inviting readers to "come out" of the Empire, it prophetically calls believers to participate in God's system-threatening resistance of the empire and to journey with God in witnessing the transformation from Babylon to Jerusalem in the here and now.

The list of cargoes mentioned in verses 11-13 is a critique of the exploitative sea trade of the Roman Empire. Finally, the court scene, where God judges the Empire for the blood of the prophets and of God's holy people, is an attempt to look at economic justice and eco-justice from the perspective of the earth and its inhabitants.

Resistance as "Disassociating and Deconstructing" the Empire's Economic System

Revelation's rhetoric of prophetic exhortation and hope becomes explicit in the twofold oracle (18: 4-8) and the call for rejoicing (18:20). The oracle and the call to rejoice to pronounce the sentence on Babylon reveal God's determination to bring justice to the victims of imperial plunder and exploitation.[3] Rossing further points out that the exhortation "come out of her, my people" invokes the Exodus motif. Just as the Hebrew Bible refers to the exodus of the Israelites from Egypt, or Babylon (Jer 50:8; 51:6,45), this call encourages the people of God to leave the Great City that in 11:8 has been called Sodom and Egypt.[4] Since the figure of Babylon represents not only the city of Rome but the whole of the Roman Empire, the call to "come out of it" must be understood metaphorically as a call to depart from Rome's injustice, idolatry and murder.[5]

Revelation's theological rhetoric is not merely a call for revenge or punishment but a prophetic invitation to join in the mission to challenge the exploitative economy of the empire and an attempt towards a reversal or for an alternative religious and economic life.

The South Asian People's Action on Climate Crisis (SAPACC) is one the best examples of people's movements which resist development projects that affect the earth and the poor. This movement is comprised of farmers' organisations, trade union federations, indigenous people's organisations, fisher groups, women's organisations, and environmental groups from Bangladesh, Nepal, Sri Lanka and India.[6]

Disassociating from the Empire's Economic System

"Come out of her" is one of the central themes of Revelation. By saying "come out," John does not directly mean a geographical exodus from the Roman city but an economic, socio-political and religious disassociation from the Roman imperial order. According to Richard Bauckham, the verse, "Come out of her, my people, so that you do not take part in her sins, and so that you do not share in her plagues (Revelation 18:4)" could have been borrowed from Jeremiah 51:45 (Come out of her, my people! Save your lives, each of you, from the fierce anger of the Lord!). For Bauckham, it is not meant in a literal geographical sense as in Jeremiah, because none of John's first readers lived in the city of Rome. The command is for the readers to disassociate themselves from Rome's evil lest they shared their guilt and punishment.[7]

Deconstructing the Empire's Economic System

> And the merchants of the earth weep and mourn for her since no one buys their cargo anymore, cargo of gold, silver, jewels and pearls, fine linen, purple, silk and scarlet, all kinds of scented wood, all articles of ivory, all articles of costly wood, bronze, iron, and marble, cinnamon, spice, incense, myrrh, frankincense, wine, olive oil, choice flour and wheat, cattle and sheep, horses and chariots, slaves and human lives. (Revelation 18:11-13)

Bauckham asserts that John derives the whole of chapter 18 from the Old Testament prophecies of the fall of Babylon and Tyre. Though John borrows phrases, images and ideas, John creates a fresh prophecy, which is seen in three groups of mourners for Babylon (verses 9-19). Most importantly, Bauckham focuses on the prominence that John gives to the "merchandise" imported to Rome. To an extent, John wishes that this imported wealth will also perish with the city during its fall.

We need to give special attention to John's list of twenty-eight items of merchandise imported by the sea which significantly shows Revelation's polemic against Rome.[8] This list is modelled on Ezekiel's list of forty foreign products in which the city of Tyre traded (Ez 27:12-24).[9]

Bauckham gives a detailed analysis of the list of the different cargoes and the places from where these imports were made—gold, silver and wine from Spain, precious stones from India, pearls from the Red Sea and India, fine linen from Egypt, purple from the Mediterranean, scarlet from Kermes Oaks, citrus wood from the North African Coast, ivory from North Africa, costly wood from Africa and India, bronze from Corinth, iron from Spain, etc.[10]

John places slaves at the end of the list. The number of slaves one had marked the prosperity of the rich at that time. The enslavement of prisoners taken during war was one of the main sources of slaves. Rossing stresses that John wants to make it clear that slaves are not just "bodies" but living persons, they are "human life."

There are three definite classes of people, the kings of the earth, merchants of the earth (v.11), and the mariners (v. 17) who benefited from the exploitative economic system of Rome.[11] The kings might mean not only the client kings but also the local ruling classes. The "merchants of the earth" (18:3, 11) are the merchants engaged in trade with Rome from places like Puteoli, Ostia, Rome, and also from Ephesus. These merchants could also be independent shipowners who bought and sold their cargoes at the ports. The third group is the employers in the maritime transport industry (v 17).

Here John does not merely stand for the suffering Christians but stands in solidarity with all the victims of imperial oppression, including perhaps, the thousands who died in Coliseum.[12]

What we find in the "economic critique" of John is a rejection of the evil "economic omnipotence" of Rome. In mentioning the cargoes, especially, pointing to the commercial usage of human slaves, he exposes the exploitative economic power of Rome and envisions its downfall.

Coming back to SAPACC, its protest is mainly to address the exploitative economic practices and trades that cause a huge damage to the climatic situation. Their demand is for the UN to ensure that developed countries cut down their carbon emission to zero level by 2030 and developing nations by 2040. This can be done only when every country is ready to "come out" of the dominant and exploitative capitalist economic practices.

Resistance as "Upholding Justice" from the Perspective of the Victims

Resistance is not characterised by challenging the evil practices but also by fighting to ensure justice for the victims of climate change. In the context of climate change, resistance means justice to the victims of climate disasters. The rejoicing of the Christians and the heavenly court in Revelation 18 show the celebrations of the victims of the Roman Empire. Their celebration is a celebration of justice. At the same time, the oppressors are shown grieving for the loss of Babylon/Rome through the laments of merchants, shipmasters, seafarers, and sailors who were enriched by the maritime commerce of the Roman Empire.

Conclusion

Revelation chapter 18 refreshes our theological imagination and calls for courageous participation in challenging the empires of our times. It reminds us of the "never dying prophetic voices" in the midst of a hopeless and difficult situation. As we read Revelation, we are reminded of grassroots movements, many of which, like the Tamil Nadu Women's Collective mentioned in the book, highlight the presence of alternative communities that urge people to "come out" with their resistance and eco-based economics. While Revelation 18 gives a Christian theological framework for resistance, such movements provide a real prophetic witness of resistance against empire. Both the biblical text and the "real texts" of such movements in the present-day context invites us to live a life of resistance against empire and invites us to participate in the redeeming work with the earth and its inhabitants.

Endnotes

[1] Pablo Richard, *Apocalypse: A People's Commentary on the Book of Revelation.* (Maryknoll: Orbis Books), 1995.135.

[2] Ibid., 186-188.

[3] Ibid.

[4] Barbara R. Rossing, *Journeys Through Revelation: Apocalyptic Hope for Today*, Volume 23, Number 3 (Louisville: Presbyterian Women, Inc., 2010), 57.

[5] Ibid., 67.

[6] https://theecologist.org/2020/feb/26/south-asian-coalition-links-climate-social-struggles, accessed on 10 Feb 2020.

[7] Richard Bauckham. "The Economic Critique of Rome in Revelation 18." In *Images of Empire*, edited by Loveday Alexander, 47–90. Journal for the Study of the Old Testament Supplement Series 122. Sheffield, England: Sheffield Academic, 1991., 84-85.

8 Ibid., 58.

9 Ibid., 59.

10 Richard Bauckham., 60-79.

11 Richard Bauchkam., 79.

12 Nelson.J. Kraybill, *Apocalypse and Allegiance: Worship, Politics, and Devotion in the Book of Revelation.* (Grand Rapids: Brazos, 2010) 143-144.

Praying with Creation

Invocation: Flute (Meditate in Silence)

Call to Worship

P: The heavens are telling the glory of God;
and the firmament proclaims God's handiwork.

C: **Look at the birds of the air; they neither sow nor reap
nor gather into barns, and yet our heavenly parent feeds
them.**

P: Day to day pours forth speech, and night declares
knowledge.

C: **Consider the lilies of the field, how they grow;
they neither toil nor spin,
yet I tell you, even Solomon in all his glory
was not clothed like one of these.**

P: But strive first for the reign of God,
      and God's righteousness,
      and all these things will be given to you as well.

P: The grace of our Lord Jesus Christ, the Love of God
      and the sweet communion of the Holy Spirit be with
      you all.

C: **Amen**

Opening Prayer

P: Let us pray

Jesus Christ, attune us to the deep mysteries of creation.

Make our spirits sensitive to the forces of nature at work
beneath us and the suffering of those who experience these
forces when they erupt. Jesus Christ, make our hearts
sensitive to the songs of our kin, songs of celebration from
the sea, the land and the smoking mountain. Christ, teach
us to care.

C: **Amen**

Prayer of Confession

P: Let us pray (*pause*)

Creator God, the whole earth is yours and everything in
it. We acknowledge the incredible gift of our great rivers,
which provide a critical source of fresh water to our
country. The lakes are home for hundreds of native species
of fish, mammals, reptiles, birds, insects, amphibians and
plants.

C: **Creator God, we confess the harm we have done to our waters by pollution, invasive species, climate change, habitat destruction and algae blooms.**

P: Millions of people in our world live in places where the air is not safe to breathe. We cry out with all the people, many of them children, who have breathing-related sickness. But it is not only humans who are harmed when the air is toxic. Air pollution harms crops, forests, animals, soil and waterways.

C: **Creator God, we confess and lament the damage done to our skies by haze, acid rain, ozone depletion and greenhouse gas emissions.**

P: We need the soil, the seeds, the bees, the worms, the birds, and even the fungi and bacteria to make our food grow. Our countries have beautiful farmland, wetlands, forests, woodlands and urban landscapes, all of which need to be treated with respect and care.

C: **Creator God, we confess the destruction that we have wrought on land by mining, unsustainable agricultural practices, excessive waste, deforestation and erosion.**

P: For the water, the air, and the land—all of which you have called good—we pray to you, Lord. We are interconnected with all of your creation, and we grieve when any part of your creation suffers.

C: **Creator God, transform us; awaken us to action. Heal the hurts of our world, and bring our hearts to peace. Amen.**

Prayer of Thanksgiving

P: In these dark days of climate crisis, we look to those throughout the world who work to protect and restore God's good creation. In doing so, they serve God, neighbour and creation.

P: For small farmers who work tirelessly tend the land and bring forth abundance for the benefit of others.

C: **We give you thanks, O God.**

P: For the youth of the world who stand up against unjust governments that threaten the livelihood and safety of future generations.

C: **We give you thanks, O God.**

P: For environmental lawyers, legislators, activists, volunteers, and dreamers who give us hope for a better future.

C: **We give you thanks, O God.**

P: For indigenous water-protectors and native peoples across the globe who safeguard their homelands for the most vulnerable among us.

C: **We give you thanks, O God.**

P: For biologists, climate scientists, and ethicists who study and teach for the benefit of all.

C: **We give you thanks, O God.**

P: For forest protectors and conservationists who seek to protect wilderness areas and endangered wildlife.

C: **We give you thanks, O God.**

P: For the great and small actions of the many who work to reduce climate impact.

C: **We give you thanks, O God.**

ALL: **O God, we give thanks for the many across the globe who work against the careless destruction of our shared natural resources. Their work is their prayer for a better future for all of humanity and animal kind. May they be an example to us of what it means to have dominion over the earth. Bless their work today and always.**

Gathering Bhajan or Hymn

Scripture Reading

Leviticus 25: 1-7

Psalm 24

Matthew 6:25-34

Affirmation of Faith

P: Let us affirm our faith together.

**We believe that God creates all things,
renews all things and celebrates all things.**

**We believe that Earth is a sanctuary,
a sacred planet filled with God's presence,
a home for us to share with our kin.**

**We believe that God became flesh and blood,
became a piece of Earth,
a human being called Jesus Christ,
who lived and breathed and spoke among us,
suffered and died on a cross,
for all human beings and for all creation.**

**We believe that the risen Jesus
is the Christ at the core of creation
reconciling all things to God,
renewing all creation and filling the cosmos.**

**We believe the Spirit renews life in creation
groans in empathy with a suffering creation,
and waits with us for the rebirth of creation.**

**We believe that with Christ we will rise
and with Christ we will celebrate a new creation.**

Intercessory Prayers

P: For the well-being of creation that, while human action causes seas to rise and storms to strengthen, God might lead the tides of climate change to be turned and a healthy climate restored. Lord, in your mercy,

C: **Receive our prayer**

P: Creator God, storms rage and the oceans rise as all of your creation cries out to you. Care for your children in the face of nature's destructive power, especially those affected by floods and cyclones; comfort those who fear. Inspire those who work to conserve and protect your world. Lord, in your mercy,

C: **Receive our prayer**

P: Creator God, fishes and honeybees sing the goodness of the earth. Glaciers and deserts declare your greatness. Make us good stewards of our home for the generations to come. Lord, in your mercy,

C: **Receive our prayer**

P: Sovereign God, you raise up governments to protect the widow and the orphan. Bless citizens with wisdom and discernment as they choose leaders. Inspire leaders to always seek the common good. Lord, in your mercy,

C: **Receive our prayer**

P: We pray for all human beings that we will be filled with a spirit of concern for the future of our environment; bring an end to the exploitation of the earth's scarce resources; and live as responsible stewards protecting and respecting this gift of creation God has placed in our hands. Lord, in your mercy,

C: **Receive our prayer**

P: We pray for the organisations that are working hard to protect the climate vulnerable communities. Those who are engaged in raising awareness and building lives in disaster-prone areas and for those climate prophets who challenge the exploitative socio-economic system. Let your grace and strength prevail over them.Lord, in your mercy,

C: **Receive our prayer**

P: We pray for those who have lost their lives due to climate disasters. Let their memories continue to haunt us so that as we remember them, we will also commit to work to save the lives of innocent people in the future. Lord, in your mercy,

C: Receive our prayer

(More supplications can be added.)

Lord's Prayer

Commissioning

P: Go out into creation

Experience creation in its vast beauty and diversity

Stand in awe of the work of God's hands

Have courage to stand in the way of destruction

Go out to be faithful servants of the earth

Love the Lord your God

With all your heart

With all your soul

With all your mind

And serve the creation God has given us.

C: Amen

Blessing

You were made for this earth,
and this earth was made for you.

Go forth to love and serve it,
knowing in your deepest heart
that you are blessed from the beginning of time.
In the name of the One
who called all things good.
Amen.

Parts of this liturgy was used in the Seasons of Creation Worship at the Lutheran School of Theology at Chicago.

Commissioning Adapted from *This Far By Faith*

Call to Worship adapted from https://www.united-church.ca/worship-theme/environment

Afterword

*Lalrindiki Ralte**

The DARE programme, which engages us to reimagine church as an event that happens in particular contexts in the life of communities longing for love, freedom, dignity, justice, acceptance and flourishing of life, has to be born out of the concerns of life in concrete socio-economic and political realities. This is necessary in order to create space for the development of faith communities whose mission is to usher in the reign of God in the midst of death and destruction.

In the context of South Asia, the climate crisis has created a situation which not only makes life uncomfortable and inconvenient for all, but has become a survival issue of the poor and vulnerable groups and communities all across the region. In such a situation. the book *Church and Climate Change* written by Vinod Wesley provides an important tool for the local faith communities to discern the factors responsible for the present situation as well as to understand the interlinkages between faith and climate change.

Even though climate change has created devastating effects in local communities, many religious people, including local church congregations, seem to be unaware of or are indifferent to the connection between their faith and the environmental crisis that they are facing. Wesley has identified two approaches with strong theological justifications that compartmentalise faith and social realities. He calls one group as 'climate change deniers' and the other as 'conservative evangelicals' who refuse to acknowledge the reality of climate change and the role of human beings in bringing about this catastrophe. The former denies that there is a problem with the environment and they justify the destructive actions of human beings against nature on the grounds that human beings are given authority by God to have dominion over the rest of creation.. The latter simply equates the different manifestations of climate change, such as plagues, earthquakes, severe floods and ecological disasters, as a sign of the "end times." The author criticises these approaches by pointing out that they are unable to link the present ecological destruction and climate change with sinful greed and the exploitative capitalist economic system. Their interpretation of the Bible to justify their theological stand is also against several biblical passages which affirm that God cares for the whole creation and that human beings are called to participate in caring for the earth as well.

Thus, climate change is not merely an economic issue but also a religio-political and theological issue. A different approach to climate change is needed to make people to overcome their indifferences and transcend their conservative theological orientation. Wesley proposes a justice-oriented approach, which takes seriously authentic and reliable scientific reports about the danger of environmental destruction and a spiritual commitment to save the earth and the poor by challenging the capitalist economic structure. He builds upon his proposal with biblical and theological interpretations and affirmations drawn from the works of scholars who have deep compassion for God's good creation, who are critical of the dominant capitalist economic system and who advocate the role of human beings as caretakers and stewards of the rest of creation.

In South Asian countries, the structural violence of patriarchy and exploitation of their labour make women to be much more adversely affected by climate change. However, women are not merely victims. Many of them are actively responding to climate change and injustice through theological and theoretical discourses as well as with many practical examples from their experiences inside houses and outside. Wesley has brought out the impact of climate change on women in an insightful and sensitive manner.

Theological reflection and affirmation need practical engagement/s to bring about a radical change for the better. Wesley has cited the works of climate activists, mostly young people, in South Asian countries like Bangladesh and India as well as in other Asian countries and also at the international level. Some of them have taken up issues on how climate change is enforcing the oppression of women and children, some organise strikes to raise awareness and to protest against destructive development projects, some of them join the struggle of indigenous communities who are trying to protect their land and forest against business corporations, and some are involved in the struggle to include lessons about climate change in the school curriculum. These are important pointers for local congregations that may want to engage more fully in the work of justice, particularly in ensuring climate justice, and in the process free themselves from unjust, rigid and indifferent faith community orientation and practices.

In the multireligious and multicultural South Asian context, climate change cannot be the concern of one faith community alone. People of different faiths need to discover their own faith traditions which can inspire them to theologically respond to climate change. They need to come together, bringing their rich and diverse sources, to affirm the goodness of the whole creation and to commit themselves to struggle together against the destructive neoliberal capitalist economic policy. There may also be people of no faith but who have a deep sense of justice for the whole creation. Such people can become part of the faith movements committed to bring about climate justice. By participating actively in such movements, the church can truly become an event that gives birth to enduring ecumenism and inclusive communities.

We are now living in a world where every aspect of our lives is disrupted by the deadly COVID-19 pandemic. In a joint statement issued titled "Calling for an Economy of Life in a Time of Pandemic" issued by the World Council of Churches (WCC), the World Communion of Reformed Churches (WCRC), the Lutheran World Federation (LWF), and the Council for World Mission (CWM), a clear and decisive connection is made between the spread of the virus and the relentless exploitation and destruction of different species and the ecosystem by the extractive neoliberal economic system. The plundering and exploitation of resources and other species by human beings create an ideal environment for all kinds of diseases and viruses to spill over. Urbanisation and globalisation further aggravate the rapid spread of the virus to all corners of the world within a short period of time. The already vulnerable people, such as workers in the informal sectors, the poor, women, people of colour, migrants and indigenous communities, bear the brunt of it all in terms of loss of lives and livelihoods.

The DARE programme of CWM has already played a prophetic and midwifery role in preparing local faith communities to respond meaningfully and creatively to this kind of unprecedented pandemic which is related to climate change. In this time of uncertainties and fears, books like this can become crucial resources for igniting the passion for engagement among local communities that need to be strengthened theologically and practically to rise up to the challenges of the day.

* **The Dr. Lalrindiki Ralte** serves the Aizwal Theological College, Aizwal, Mizoram as Associate Professor. Prior to that, she served the Senate of Serampore College (University) as Dean for Extension Programme.

Bibliography

Abraham K.C. "A Theological Response to the Ecological Crisis," in *Ecotheology: Voices from South and North*, edited by David G. Hallman. New York: WCC/Orbis books, 1994.

Abraham K.C. *Eco-Justice: A New Agenda for Church's Mission*. Allahabad: Servisage, 2000.

Abraham K.C. *Transforming Vision: Theological–Methodological Paradigm Shifts*. Tiruvalla: CSS, 2006.

Antal, Jim. *Climate Church Climate World: How People of Faith must Work for Change*. New York: Rowman& LittleField, 2018.

Aruna Gnanadason, "The Struggle to Survive: Women and Environmental Justice–A Theological Response," in *Religion and Society*, Vol. 56 No. 3-4, Sept-Dec. 2011. 48.

Bauckham, Richard. "The Economic Critique of Rome in Revelation 18," in *Images of Empire*, edited by Loveday Alexander, Sheffield: Sheffield Academic, 1991.

Bauckham, Richard. *The Climax of Prophecy: Studies on the Book of Revelation*. Edinburg: T&T Clark, 1993.

Bauckham, Richard. *The Theology of the Book of Revelation*. Cambridge: Cambridge University Press, 1993.

Bloomquist, Karen L. (ed.). *God, Creation and Climate Change. Spiritual and Ethical Perspectives.*Geneva: LWF Studies, 2009.

Bloomquist, Karen L. "What do You See, Feel, Believe in the face of Climate Change," in *God, Creation and Climate Change. Spiritual and Ethical Perspectives*. edited by Karen L. Bloomquist, Geneva: LWF Studies, 2009.

Boring, M. Eugene. *Revelation: Interpretation Bible Commentary.* Louisville: John Knox Press, 1989.

Damiel D. Chetti, *Ecology and Development: Theological Perspectives.* Madras, UELCI/Gurukul/ BTESSC, 1991.

Delgado, Sharon. *Love in a Time of Climate Change: Honoring Creation, Establishing Justice.* Minneapolis: Fortress Press, 2017.

Dietrich, Gabriele. *A New Thing on Earth.* Delhi: ISPCK, 2001.

Dietrich, Gabriele. "Ethnicity, Ecology & Feminism," in *AJTR*, VI, 1, Jan-June, 1993

Dietrich, Gabriele. "Women's Perspective on Ecology," in *Religion and Society*, Vol. XXXVII, No.2, June 1990.

Gebara, Iveone. "The Trinity and Human Experience: An Ecofeminist approach," in *Women Healing Earth: Third World Women on Ecology, Feminism, and Religion.* edited by Rosemary Radford Ruether. New York: Orbis Books, 1996.

Gorringe, Timothy. "The Trinity," in *Systematic Theology and Climate Change: Ecumenical Perspectives*, edited by Michael S. Northcott and Peter M. Scott. New York: Routledge, 2014.

Gregersen, Neils Henrik. "Christology," in *Systematic Theology and Climate Change: Ecumenical Perspectives,* edited by Michael S. Northcott and Peter M. Scott. New York: Routledge, 2014.

Gregorios, Paulos. *The Human Presence: An Orthodox View of Nature.* Geneva: World Council of Churches, 1978.

Habel, Norman C, David Rhoads and H. Paul Santmire (eds.), *The Season of Creation: A Preaching Commentary.* Minneapolis: Fortress Press, 2011.

Habel, Norman C. and Peter Trudinger (eds). *Exploring Ecological Hermeneutics.* Atlanta: Society of Biblical Literature, 2008.

Harris. Melanie L. *Ecowomanism: African American Women and Earth-Honoring Faiths.* Maryknoll: Orbis Books, 2017.

Ilaiah, Kancha. *Post-Hindu India.* New Delhi: Sage Publication, 2006.

Ji-Sun Kim, Grace and Hilda P. Koster (eds.) *Planetary Solidarity: Global Women's Voice on Christian Doctrine and Climate Justice.* Minneapolis: Fortress Press, 2017.

Martin-Schramm, James B. *Climate Justice: Ethics, Energy, and Public Policy.* Fortress Press: Minneapolis, 2010.

McFague, Sallie. *A New Climate for Theology: God, The World, and Global Warming*. Minneapolis: Fortress Press, 2008.

McFague, Sallie. *A New Climate for Theology*. Minneapolis: Fortress Press, 2008.

Moe-Lobeda, Cynthia. *Resisting Structural Evil: Love as Ecological- Economic Vocation*. Minneapolis: Fortress Press, 2013.

Moe-Lobeda, Cynthia. "Cross, Resurrection and the Indwelling God," in *God, Creation and Climate Change: Spiritual and Ethical Perspectives*, edited by Karen L. Bloomquist. Geneva: LWF Studies, 2009.

Nalunnakkal, Geevarghese Coorilos. *Ethical Issues: Subaltern Perspectives*. Tiruvalla: CSS 2007.

Quinn, Frederick. *To Heal the Earth: A Theology of Ecology*. Nashville: Upper Room Books, 1994.

Rasmussen, Larry L. *Earth Community Earth Ethics*. New York: Orbis Books, 1996.

Richard, Pablo. *Apocalypse: A People's Commentary on the Book of Revelation*. Maryknoll: Orbis Books, 1995.

Rowthorn, Anne. *Caring for Creation*. Wilton: Morehouse Publishing,1989.

Samuel Rayan, "The Earth is the Lord's," in *Ecotheology: Voices from South and North,* edited by David G. Hallman. New York: WCC/Orbis books, 1994.

Singh, Ivy. "Eco-feminism as a Paradigm Shift in Theology," in IJT 45/1&2, 2003.

Stueckelberger, Christoph. "Who Dies First? Who is Sacrificed First? Ethical Aspects of Climate Justice," in *God, Creation and Climate Change. Spiritual and Ethical Perspectives,* edited by Karen L. Bloomquist. Geneva: LWF Studies, 2009.

Tamara Grdzelidze, "The Church," in *Systematic Theology and Climate Change: Ecumenical Perspectives, edited by Michael S. Northcott and Peter M. Scott* (New York: Routledge, 2014)

Thompson, Milburn J. *Justice and Peace: A Christian Primer (Third Edition)*. New York: Orbis Books, 2019.

Victus, Solomon. "Key Hurdles of Eco-Theology in Theological Discourse," in *Margins in Conversation: Methodological Discourses in Theological Disciplines,* edited by Mohan P. Larbeer and Joseph Prabakar Dhayam. Bangalore: BTESSC, 2012.

Victus, Solomon. "New Heaven and New Earth: Towards Climate Justice," *Religion and Society*, Vol. 56 No. 3-4, Sept-Dec. 2011.

Wielenga, Bas. *Revelation to John: Tuning into Songs of Moses and the lamb.* New Delhi: ISPCK 2009

Wilfred, Felix. *Asian Public Theology: Critical Concerns in Challenging Times.* Delhi: ISPCK, 2010.

Zachariah, George. "Discerning the Times: A Spirituality of Resistance and Alternatives," in *God Creation and Climate Change: Spiritual and Ethical Perspectives,* edited by Karen L. Bloomquist. Geneva: LWF Studies,2009.

Zachariah, George. *Alternatives Unincorporated: Earth Ethics from the Grass Roots.* London: Equinox, 2011.

Zachariah, George. *Gospel in a Groaning World: Climate Injustice and Public Witness.* Tiruvalla: CSS & NCCI, 2012.

www.ingramcontent.com/pod-product-compliance
Lightning Source LLC
LaVergne TN
LVHW090348190726